Leopardwood

Also by Malcolm McFarlane and published by Ginninderra Press
The Water Cart

Malcolm McFarlane

Leopardwood

Acknowledgements

Sincere thanks to Murray Butcher (Wilcannia) for generously reading early drafts, and for his sage advice in relation to Paarkintji language use; and also to Dr Chris Sarra and Jack Thompson AM for their incredibly generous support of my work

Leopardwood
ISBN 978 1 76109 233 6
Copyright © Malcolm McFarlane 2021

First published 2021 by
GINNINDERRA PRESS
PO Box 3461 Port Adelaide 5015
www.ginninderrapress.com.au

To Stuart Anderson, Craig Foot, Dene and Karen Griffin, and Julian and Emily Hall – many thanks, old friends, for your encouragement and advice with my scratchings over the years now many

1

just don't be a goose Arthur
don't get up in there yourself while I'm gone
yet Arthur followed the simple fence line
up to the top of the bald rocky platform
Callum's words still echoing somewhere
his friend gone a couple of hours already
there was a need to do something

see what was up there
decide
what had to be done
Arthur followed the fence
rusting incomplete wires
approaching the top
the smell began

he held tight the thick remaining metal wire
steadying his final steps
metal spikes into stone
supporting a single chain crowning the small dam wall
leaning on half taut links to grab his breath
tasting the decay of carcasses in the warm air
barely breaching the surface of the still dark pool

said Callum as he headed off to Broken Hill earlier that afternoon
lots of stuff can go wrong out here
and if something goes wrong and you're on your own
well
turning from the scene he had hiked some way to see
Arthur looked across the high boulders
back down to the thing called his new home

a homestead distant and small
yet somehow not as far away as he expected
not as far as feeble legs and beating heart would have him believe
looking rather grand from such a distance there
sweeping verandas
shaded sandstone walls
places cool

from a distance the decay and years of disarray
could not be so clearly seen
the several associated smaller tumbledown structures
surrounding the homestead proper
from a higher perch
became shapes
elegantly placed

beyond these scatterings of things
sheds large and small
a workshop
garage and the old meat safe
that smallest building there
things of stone or timber walls
corrugated-iron roofs all

beyond these structures of man
Arthur's eyes led him on a slow swoop around
where it seemed no person
had ever impacted at all
line of tall trees
though distant seemed thick and clear
betraying the path of the river's meander

strange thought Arthur quietly
no sign of the road not a hint of it
though the dirt road was there
linking communities and all properties between
on that one side of the Darling River
some telegraph poles and lazy wires
its only occasional evocation

as he turned more to the south
there were hints of soft earth roads
tracks from the homestead
fingers out to different parts of the property
yet the one fragile line he knew so far
out to the shearing shed and airstrip
not even that was plain for him to see

no glimpse from so far away
for anyone new to there
of the large raised woolshed with worn lanolin boards
Arthur wondered how much more there was there
that he simply could not see
vast as his view was
standing on a small high bundle of rocks that had somehow become a dam

the mid-afternoon heat
with its wide blue soft pale blue sky
highlighting the endless stubble of hard elegant trees
mulga and mallee
the leopardwood
a single brushstroke of white cloud
pointed to a far horizon

saltbush all around
a kind of strange heather in that landscape dry
rosemary-coloured tufts
sprinkling the pink ochre floor for miles every way
closer bushes
near the base of his pungent lookout
to his eyes simply stiff inverted witches' brooms

emerging from the saltbush clumps
disappearing again below his feet at the rocky cliff base
a simple metal pipe
the dogleg route that had enticed him
from his new worn home
to the high loose chain
to which he clung

a simple pipe
at the old homestead
putrid water dribbled after a while
the pipe he realised
must lead to the source of this problem
this possible putrefaction
and so he had set off that morning

turning again to the smell
he noticed some steps cut into rock
there followed another length of chain
hanging heavy and limp
straight down inside the rock dam wall
disappearing into dark tannin water
beside the bloated floating carcass of a kangaroo

the chain
so Callum reckoned
would be attached to some kind of chute
the thing they had discussed as priority number one
for the new owner of Leopardwood
was to pull that thing clear
drain the reservoir clean

a crime out here an absolute crime
all that precious water up there spoiled
Callum had explained earnestly
it's such a great set-up too that old rock dam thing up there
but by the foul smell of the water at the house
just no good left as it is
first task for this flash new owner I reckon

Arthur pulled on the chain with all he could give
not surprised when nothing moved
recovering his breath
he contemplated going in
anxious to ensure the water supply
impatient to feel his new life there begun
yearning for success of any kind

within him somewhere he felt a murmuring urge
complete some kind of practical task
strike the first blow
somehow feel a connection to the vastness now his
alone there a couple of days
he hoped that accomplishing just one first tangible thing
would relax or quieten him

a little away from the dead roo
dipped fingers into the brown-black pool
cool but not impossible
and it is hot up here after all
wondering about the reaction of Callum upon his return
not wanting to ignore his advice
especially now out there on country his friend knew so well

stuff it
it has to be done sometime
and it might even drain right out overnight
Arthur further rationalised
walking back down the path a little way to find a stick of any size
returning with it he poked at the sodden sad roo
so as to urge it a little away

slipping into dark cool water up there alone was one thing
but immersing himself
right next to the source of the decay
something he'd prefer to avoid
fears that the thing would disintegrate upon the first touch
unfounded
feeling it surprisingly firm Arthur pushed hard

sudden movement broke the pool's perfect smooth skin
a temporary slow wake caused
as roo blobbed ponderously towards the far end of the oval pond
several metres away
he sat to unlace boots
worn solid leather hiking boots
that in a few months had accumulated so many tales

crazy
thought he
just a few months ago
fumbling over these laces in Northern Japan
trying to undo them quickly
to step up into Hiroyuki's family home
hurrying into warm out of the snow

Arthur smiled at the unexpected journeys
urgent and now complete
removing jeans he wondered
thoughts and memories
just ambush you at times
perhaps with comfort
sometimes anguish

grasping the single vertical chain with both hands
he edged tentatively backwards into the increasing cool
submerged steps carved into rock were well formed
but after the fourth the fifth could not be found
he felt his toes scratching stupidly in the water dark and cold
a thin slime made the rock surface smooth
but then an edge jarred the numb and searching toe

the confidence of a man trying to actually get something done
so swiftly challenged
he hoped he had not broken the skin
and so chest deep in cold stale water that smelt of the decay it enclosed
he equivocated for a time
would he jump out a failure in this minor first endeavour
or take a deep breath to try to fix the thing

so often he shied away from decisiveness in any form
wondered what it was
that made him suck in less than fragrant air
push himself down
eyes flinching at the water becoming cooler
as they were hauled down
along the algae coated chain

his movement and earlier hopeless scratching at the wall
stirred up particles of long settled muck
thread globs of slime
barely able to see beyond his hands
each fumble at something created more of the same cloudy mess
Arthur gave it up and climbed out
onto the warm rock ledge wall to recover his breath and his calm

bugger it
he complained
such a possible and straightforward thing
yet a failure he had once again proved to be
madness really anyway
he reconciled
panting and reviewing his hasty plan

finding some kind of a cement plug
or perhaps metal chute long ago rusted firm
at the end of the chain
dislodging the thing
despite the pressure of all that water against it
only to feel the suck as it miraculously moved
dragging him suddenly down and further down

stinking of stale fouled water
Arthur put on jeans and boots to take another look at the outlet below
still breathing heavily he marched with haste
back down the path and around to the base
to the large stone boulders that formed the dam's front wall
looking straight up the rock face
it did seem high and his attempts foolhardy

the exfoliated convex wall arched up twenty feet or more
ageing cement roughly sealed around the emerging pipe
looking so out of place between those boulders
ancient and perfectly formed
J.M. 1954
scratched deep and clear into cement long ago wet
beside the source of the metal pipe

two large round taps
one controlling the flow heading down to the homestead
another closer to the wall an outlet release perhaps
neither would turn
neither would they turn he suspected
for someone much stronger than he
frustration fuelled his determination

he did not want this first thing
this first little task of practicality
to end in petty failure so easily
tools were few but rocks were plenty in that dry creek bed
Arthur selected a heavy stone and lifted it high above the rusting taps and pipes
the first blow bent metal down to the sandy soil
the second cracked the outlet hard up against the rock wall

cold muddy water belched out and Arthur let go a mighty cheer
beauty
you beauty
and after watching the flow for a short while
watching the dry sand of the small creek bed floor
absorb all that came its way
he headed back down that gully the way he had that morning explored

Arthur returned not to the main house
but to the shearers' quarters some distance away
the house in need of repair
still a shell of a home
unoccupied for several years
the quarters were basic but still in use for a few busy weeks each year
they would be his makeshift home for now

on the veranda of the northern block he had laid his pack
his traveller's bag of belongings from which he hoped would grow a home
two parallel simple dormitories
each with five single rooms
separated at one end by the kitchen block with showers and toilets over behind
in the centre of the dusty open quadrangle this formed
the centrepiece fireplace with a collection of fixed timber seats all around

Arthur added some kindling he had collected along his return walk back down
contributing to the pile of large cut wood left by someone some time before
felt the smooth weight of even the small branches of these dry-country trees
making a fire in the half-barrel metal hearth as the shadows lengthened
as the hot autumn day cooled
sensed some comfort and calm within his lonely surrounds
simply because a fire was now there

sausages cooked on the rough hotplate and eaten with soft white bread
washed down with mugs of tea
the rainwater tank next to the kitchen was large and quite new
to be safe though he boiled up the cast-iron kettle again
there'd be drinking water for the morning
rolled several cigarettes and smoked them
dark and the sharp cool set in

alone except for the fire
alone except for his memories and plans
so many bad things and days sad that had been
and now
through some crazy few months of luck and fate
he could ponder things he might actually achieve
I need to give up the smokes too thought Arthur as sleep was attempted

the old single bed stiff and narrow
but within sleeping bag he was at least warm
too much tobacco left a furry bitterness in his mouth
a slight ache spin to his head
he glimpsed the embers of the fire fading
though a little far away to benefit from its warmth
the glow was company

waking at dawn he rekindled the flames,
drowsy memories or dreams
the sounds of roos
soft thumping nearby
dogs were they howling it seemed all around
tea and bread and he was on his way
anxious to check the dam

first signs were good
from a long way off he could see evidence of damp
water had tumbled along the creek bed
before soaking through the thick sand
a mob of birds at the foot of the wall
galahs hawks and crows
and a few smaller finches of some kind he did not recognise

all were squawking in competition for the shrinking pool
the two-inch muddy flow of the day before
had at some time since blown out to a hole a foot or so wide
cement around the pipe had totally given way
just below where J.M. had made his mark several decades before
the flow now long ceased he bent down attempting to see up through the hole
but there was no daylight on the other side

crap and lots of it
including that old roo no doubt
Arthur mumbled as he made his way along the path's high curve up and around
the stench was the same
but thicker than the day before
though with no idea how he would clean it out and now patch the thing
he at least felt that progress had been made

a little clumsy for sure but at least he had begun
made his way up eagerly to the final chain
Arthur's heart sank a little though at what he saw
sludge and slime glistened on the concave walls on either side
below him amid the pitch-soaked brambles
clogging up the sudden drain hole against the joined kissing boulders
the carcasses of three roos and several tangles of bones from beasts beyond decay

again he wanted to descend the carved rock stairs
but it could not be
the chain pinned tight against the hard stone
whatever plug thing attached jammed tight below the mess of debris
instead of chancing the carved slimy steps
he walked around the other side of the dam's perimeter
though it did not look like a dam any more

begun already to appear
he supposed
as it would have before 1954
when whoever J.M. was decided to patch those rocky caves
block up the boulder wall
Arthur made his way upstream
to where the creek would enter the dam when it flowed

from there he looked up into the cavern so long unseen
muck had already mostly oozed down to the soupy muddy narrow floor
as he peered up to one side of the overhang
clear cool light of an autumn morning
began to make shadows of the thin scrub above on the long damp wall
he thought there seemed to be the shape of a kangaroo
right there on the sheltered rock face before him

just a trick of the early light surely
he looked down to the dam wall end
the upturned bloated stinking carcass in a fog of black flies
wondered how it and the other objects of decay met their demise
Arthur looked though again up at the wall
saw another rough shape in relief of a roo
and there an emu and some straight lines and curves symmetrical all

a shiver he felt descend his spine
made out the shape of a larger emu and a bird
perhaps an eagle
looking across excitedly at the opposing overhang cave
all was in shadow still
slipping on the putrid mud beneath his feet
he hurriedly crossed to the other side

more of the same
symmetrical curves and parallel lines
small figures standing
Arthur found himself running a few paces quickly away
then stopping and turning back to face the whole scene
slumping down onto haunches on that unhappy ground
from where he gazed and deeply sighed

2

Callum entered the bar to the shrill fluorescent sounds of poker machines
the gaudy carpet of yellow black and green swirls
unchanged in his three years away
though more worn and beer sticky
hoping to find Harry already there
and he was
in full throttle at a corner table with three other men

all wore the same khaki power company badged shirts
Callum approached his friend and these men unknown
all except Harry were draining schooner glasses and rising as if to leave
they departed amid one loud final laugh shared
spotting Callum heading his way
Harry stood up and offered his large firm hand
hey there and how about a beer eh

you're looking pretty settled in
I'll get these
Callum was always pleased to catch up with Harry
just the second time he'd seen him since his return to Broken Hill
it was as it is with true old friends
as though he had never departed at all
two large amber beers he brought to the table

cheers young fella offered Harry
good to see you too old man smiled Callum
they drank some
having to huddle a little over the small round table to be heard
to try to converse above the late Friday afternoon melee
a month or so before when they had met over at Tilpa
the talk was mostly of Callum and his travels

typical of Harry
thought Callum
more interested in others than himself
as a kid he'd looked up to Harry always
the big strong gentle friend of his older brother
and now so well respected and known
a Paarkintji man

Callum looked at how the years had and had not changed Harry
now in his thirties
large frame bulkier but very solid still
mop of crazy curly hair gone
totally shaved
the smooth dark brown dome
so intimidating on some

yet with Harry seemed to further enhance
round friendly face and cheeky eyes
Callum wanted to hear his stories from the past few years
so much no doubt had also happened to him
but that evening they both had another very recent yarn in mind
so how's he going out there do ye reckon
our new fella

asked Harry with his broad happy grin
Arthur you mean Callum checked eagerly
glad to know that Harry's interest was there
yeah Arthur the millionaire
seems like a hell of a nice bloke mind
pretty quiet though eh
not flash with it so it seems

so how do you know he's a millionaire
quizzed Callum though he knew it to be true
mate his friend countered confidently
no one comes out here and just
just puts money down on a block like Leopardwood there
straight away no questions
without having a bit behind them

christ
he didn't even have a proper geek at the river before he wanted to sign
I was there
and you too
what's the go with him
Callum sighed and put his glass down on the small circular table
wondering what and how well he could explain

like I said over at Tilpa the other day
I met him in Japan a few months back
just before I was about to leave
seems he'd hooked up with a Japanese mate of mine
while he was in Port Moresby
Papua New Guinea
Arthur there just travelling around

Hiroyuki was a mate from where I was working way up in the north
in PNG Hiroyuki was working on some government job
Arthur just travelling around
you know
and anyhow my mate over there in Japan
Sam from New York and I
we were planning a trip to China just before I'm about to head home

along comes Hiroyuki with Arthur in tow
on one of our last nights in Akita
up in northern Japan where I was teaching
Sam suddenly invites old mate to come along
too much sake at the time
but it turned out all right
the three of us spent a month kickin' around China

he's a good bloke
but a bit quiet I guess
at which point Harry quizzed some more
and so where does all the dosh come from
he doesn't seem like the type
you know what I mean
not up himself at all

hell no
and here's the thing
and I'll tell you Harry
but I don't know
not sure how much
he wants this to be common knowledge
you with me

yeah yeah I'll be tight it's right
Harry looked at Callum with genuine concentration
there was a puzzle he wanted to solve
Callum paused but only briefly
knowing that a secret told to Harry was in very safe hands
well
he began again

he'll probably share all this with you one day himself
because I reckon he'll get to know you and me both pretty well
he needs to get to know us well I reckon
not knowing this part of the world at all
not totally impractical
spent most of his time in sawmills so he said
but he's from the coast see

never been beyond the sandstone curtain before this I don't reckon
Harry broke in
laughing at his friend
but the money
what about the money
Callum smiled at his impatient friend
continuing with a little more haste

well this is the thing
there we were in China
right up the backblocks too mind you
fascinating bloody place
and he suddenly one day just blurts it all out
we'd had a pretty rough day pretty full-on
up in Tibet

Sam my New York mate as always leading the way
we've gotta do this experience that
to the point that we found out where there was a sky burial
where they chop up their dead and feed them to the birds
Harry looked at his friend in disbelief
say what
chop up their people you mean

yeah full on they do Callum continued
*there were four bodies
one of them only a kid too which was hard
laid out in the open on this kind of rock platform
not too far from a temple or monastery
very spiritual and all that but when it came down to it
there were bodies being chopped up in front of us*

*then all these birds
crows first
then vultures and eagles
god it was something
anyhow
we all felt really weird just being there
angry at a couple of other guys too*

*some other Westerners who were taking photos all through
even though you were not supposed to
a priest fella had come over to us before
and with signs and a few words made it clear
no photos of what was about to unfold
but one bloke snapped away happily sneaky like
ignorantly*

*then the other thing that got Arthur
was that when we left
when we wanted to go
the three of us took this path
just looked like any other track to me
but holy hell did the locals have a go at us then
throwing rocks and shouting and carrying on*

we legged it without understanding what it was that had offended them
just feeling you know real bad
Harry listened intently
amazed at what Callum was offering him
trying to imagine how the thin young fella
the boy he had play wrestled out on their old farm years ago
could possibly have seen what he had seen

Callum in turn could see the effect of his words on his friend
continuing
well it got to all of us a bit I guess
felt like pig ignorant Westerners and all that
but then
as we were poking around later that day
looking at all these amazing other places and things

Arthur
suddenly blurts out all this stuff
how his seven million dollars
is never going to undo the wrong they did that day
he was really upset eh
Sam and I just looked at him
he was full-on sobbing and carrying on for a while

you get to know people pretty well pretty quickly
travelling around like we were
we thought he was just trying to travel cheap like us you know
taking some time out for a while
then after a few minutes
he starts to explain
like the floodgates had opened I guess

all this stuff
his wife had died
he hit the bottle and lost his job then his home
spent a year or so on the streets
then one night he comes across a young woman in the park
pretty beaten up and left for dead
so he helps her

gets hold of a copper and stuff
then months later she suddenly turns up again
tracked him down to try to thank him
gives him a week all expenses paid at a flash hotel at the beach
and a lottery ticket
well the lottery ticket's the big one
seven mil

Harry plonked his glass down on the table
well stuff me eh
and he let out a whoop of a cheer
how would you be
from the streets to millionaire
christ almighty
he smiled as he drank from his beer

as Callum continued
yeah it's pretty full-on
and only a few months ago too
it's still eating at him I reckon
you know
Callum wondered how he may better explain
thoughts not yet clear in his own mind

well yeah Harry added with his deep giggle returning
but a pretty good problem to have eh
to which Callum responded more seriously
yeah sure but it's freaked him out a bit too I reckon
he really badly wants to do something good with the stuff
doesn't want to mess it up
such an unexpected and amazing chance

to which his friend fell silent for a moment
then asked
but why out here
christ he could keep travelling the world
get some flash place in Sydney
make some donations here and there
not like he can't do good in comfort

why on 75,000 acres
he won't last will he the large man determined
I dunno Harry
he's a funny one
he just may do
I was heading home after China
and I could see he was over travelling already

not just that sky burial thing in Tibet either
he didn't want to become one of these rambling
jaded travellers you sometimes see
totally rootless
not contributing anything
but he didn't have a clue what to do
still doesn't maybe

but something clicked with him out here straight away
when we went our separate ways in Shanghai
I suggested he come and visit out here
when he was done with tripping around
well no sooner did I get home and he was here
Harry sat back in his chair
amazed by all he had heard

maybe out here he's also escaping stuff still
we have our fair share of people hiding
hiding out in all this open space
smiling as he rubbed his bald dark head
well yeah there's probably a bit in that too
Callum readily agreed
he didn't want to come over today

said he wanted to know what it was like
to be there by himself
but I think he wanted to stay off the grog too
he's been talking for a couple of days now
about not drinking any more
and at this Harry laughed
jesus he was giving it a fair shake at Tilpa the other day

at Tilpa pub he was fairly leading the charge
he's got a taste for it if you ask me
one too many and two not enough
to which Callum jeered
yeah like a couple of others I know
your shout too ya bludger by the way
he instructed amid more knowing grins

returning with glasses brim full
a packet of nuts to share
Harry was eager to learn more
and so you said on the phone
you were going back over tomorrow
back to Leopardwood
to help him some more

yeah and I've got quite a shopping list too
I start back at the school in a few weeks
after the Easter break
so I'm happy to give him a hand while I can
Callum shook his head and smiled in disbelief as he explained
apart from the usual supermarket long list
he's given me a few other blank cheques and all

now you're talkin buddy
where shall we go eh Harry jibed
none of your corruption here mate
Callum exaggerated
my instructions are clear
the purchase of a decent ute trailer and two trail bikes
all done too

be ready to pick up by lunchtime tomorrow
then I'm heading back over
it'd be nice to have money wouldn't it
Harry laughed out loud
way to go Arthur
well if you've got it to spend
bloody hell eh get into it

yeah but get this Callum continued hastily
he's got no licence
lapsed of course while he was sleeping rough
and he hasn't been on a bike in years
so he reckons two would be good
a bit of company
why don't you come over too eh Harry

I told him I was going to try to hook up with you tonight
you working tomorrow
Harry grinned at the thought
no not till Tuesday now
tell you what
I want to see my boy tomorrow
so I'll swing by on Sunday eh

you can have those shiny new bikes warmed up by then
might even throw in the guns
knock over a roo eh
but then you'd better tell me
do millionaires eat wallaby stew
at which they succumbed to laughter
and one more round of beers

3

Arthur's night had been largely without cheer
the fire he made to lift his spirits
far larger than required
the night was clear with just a faint shaft of a crescent moon
stars like he had never encountered
before arriving at his new home
breathtaking across the entire globe it seemed

bacon and eggs on soft white bread
the last of the food he had bought from the Tilpa pub
strong black tea with lots of sugar
the way he had learned to drink it in PNG
chill of the autumn air again surprised him
the hot dry west not a place he expected to find such cool
he put off sleep though truly tired

instead he poked at the coals and stoked the fire some more
amazed by the heat the mulga wood threw
such a heavy dense slow-growing tree
once under way its fire was a jewel of a thing
more tea and cigarettes rolled
delayed closing his eyes
from fear he might see endlessly those carvings in rock

those shapes etched by hands
who knows how long before being left to drown
now in that cool night air
due to him the water gone
exposed and supporting sludge
cupping slime
what was J.M. thinking he wondered as he wrestled with sleep

creating a dam
from the collection of rocks that were for eons there
would have been one huge effort certainly
yet forming up that space
drowning that special space
so that water was secure and on tap for a few
something he could not comprehend

how did they feel
in 1954 and thereafter
observing a downpour long-awaited
immersing works of art
would there have been paintings too
washed away now
sleep did not come easily

despite his shower in the clean tank water
Arthur still sensed the stale smell of the dam
on his skin and in his hair
dogs again menaced occasionally between patches of sleep
somewhere afar in the deep cold air
until morning when he found himself walking
filling in time until Callum's return

eager to tell him
share with him the disturbing find
Callum would have an idea
Callum would know what to do
he would be back in the afternoon
Arthur walked to the river
about a kilometre from his shearers' quarters home

hiking boots
his boys' own adventure chunky boots
gave a sense of security
on what felt like such foreign ground still
the bush to Arthur his whole life
had been a thing lush
the forests and hills of the coastal fringe

walking here was a different thing
so open the country
so sparse the vegetation on the ground
he followed the worn path of an animal unknown
towards the wooded line that was the river ahead
conscious of snakes
eyes scanning the ground

so many signs of things passing even to his untrained eyes
scratchings of feet small and tails dragged
through the soft orange-pink soil
in places the ground rocky and coarse
then again the dry earth as fine as sifted flour
a shingleback lizard took off in front of him
Arthur jumped a little then laughed at his own nervous fragility

just as he was enjoying the walk
soaking in all he could see
a dumpy little harmless lizard
rattled his confidence and moment of calm
he watched the thing scamper a little away
to the shelter of dead branches and leaves fallen below an old mallee tree
such a prehistoric-looking thing

its skin hard dark lumpy scales
the head a diamond solid thing
not a foot away from the nothing stubby tail
a true desert creature
now shared his property
or rather
he its piece of land

Arthur figured
if he walked to the river and headed back along upstream for a while
he would have most of the morning utilised
he could have been busying himself
with any one of a number of things at the quarters
or at the main house complex
but where to begin

the enormity of stuff to do
somehow strangely made it easier to not even begin
he needed to get to know his land
or so he rationalised the morning away
the steepness of the river bank amazed him
just as it had when he and Callum pulled up at Tilpa
some weeks before

his first proper sight of the Darling
after a brief buffer of light brush
the elegantly gnarled river red gum trees
the bank was there
falling straight away down at forty-five degrees
so far to the water
the silty cream barely flowing stream

he wanted to go down
so picked a way carefully along the sometimes firm then loamy bank
his steps followed scents of a dry moist breeze
carrying the breath of generations upon unresolved air
lingering at the back of a parched throat
with the taste of a dry river bed swirling in a nothing breeze
distilling through the arid eucalypt and banks of sand

water was cool on his fingertips as he stroked at it
patting it briefly
attempting to not wet his boots
where crumbling sand moistened into a slurry at the water's edge
he wondered at this colour
light brown sandstone cream
flowing beside him

since he had arrived there
everyone had mentioned the rise that was coming down
he understood how the water pushed slowly down
even from rains in Queensland
but there was none of that yet to see
crazy thing really thought he
how could a river rise with no sign of rain

looking back up the bank
twenty metres or so easily
across to the other side perhaps fifty metres away
he wondered if those banks could ever be filled really
so much water
on such a clear dry day
seemed close to an impossibility

there was a sameness after a time
as he ambled along the top of the high bank edge
a regularity to the riverbank
yet every square foot seemed to intrigue
huge red gums in one place solid and set well back
at others defying gravity on the edge of the steep bank
roots long exposed

he sat for a while atop the trunk of one long fallen
crown dead and pointing down
drooping down to the stream it almost joined
long fingers of olive eucalypt leaves
so nearly touching the barely moving milk coffee stream
this flaccid thing supposed to be a mighty river
within a continent huge and dry

Arthur sat in the sun
becoming almost too warm on top of the large fallen log
he tried again to imagine the rise in the water
those leaves would be moist soon he supposed
the log too would be moved elsewhere
if stories of such water were true
one rolled cigarette was followed by a second

I really need to give these away
he mumbled as he pushed tired legs up the bank
the steep crumbling bank
his mouth tobacco-bitter and dry
lungs struggling in the dry air
Arthur walked along the bank some more
keen to find another track of some kind

back out to the more open ground and then home
he figured that all going well Callum might even be back soon
gradually he realised that he needed water
needed to drink yet the river too murky
with some anxiety he continued on his uncertain way
for a time the tracks all seemed to run parallel to the flow
then down the bank a criss-cross of meanders scattering

then a few paces more
just as he was wondering
if he should not return the way he came
he spotted the pump station in front of him
the upright engine's paint of racing green
coated in a fine dust film
also many a spot of dark grey

grease
diesel or oil
collected anything that might be in the air
creating a shadow
proof of use
proof of effort and energy expended
a feature of the silent machine

a simple flat tin roof
supported by metal fence post uprights
attempted to shelter the engine exposed
a surprisingly quite new and full 44-gallon drum of diesel stood beside
with a heavy smooth crank handle
hanging over its smeared round top
Arthur held the heavy object in his hands

fitting it to its shaft briefly
as if to give himself confidence
that he could operate the thing when the time came
he replaced the handle back on top of the drum
feeling the grease now on his hands
smelling them for their scents
oil and diesel and cold metal

the silent engine sat on a metal sleigh contraption
waiting either to be kicked into life
or dragged off disconnected
behind a tractor just ahead of a full-banking river on the rise
the bank here had become a mess of erosion
the intake pipe leading from the pump
disappearing beneath the remains of the shallow water below

its own little untidy gully around the straight pipe
right the way down
these metal objects resting
on the otherwise fragile bank's soil
seemed to create more tracks and reasons for wash-aways
Arthur decided to follow the worn vehicle track beside the pipe
surely it would simply lead back home

the slim metal pipe
here and there lost in drifts of sandy soil
only to re-emerge each time a few yards further on
Arthur stuck to the track worn by vehicles over years
a lone small kangaroo tested his nerves
deciding to jump right before him and away
as the stranger disturbed its slumber in a patch of cool sand and shade

Arthur could soon see the signs of the homestead above
flat harsh patchy scrub
some taller trees and the slim high fragile metal windmill caught his eye
once clear in his mind where he was
he left the track
cut across to the shearers' quarters
and the cool water he knew to be there

seeing Callum and the new vehicles already there surprised him
though he had wandered some way
from the scattering of buildings
somehow thought
he would have heard anyone
cross the metal ramp from the road
scatter that loose dry gravel

he smiled to himself
not even the sounds of things do I understand here
Callum was loosening the straps on the trailer
beaming at the load as his friend approached
this pair should do the job mate eh
he threw an unfastened strap across the trailer
loaded with jerrycans of fuel and two new blue and white motorbikes

you'd think so yeah
Arthur headed straight past him and into the courtyard
poured water from the large kettle into mug
beside the cold fireplace
mug filled
attempting to quaff it down
while hopefully disguising his thirst from Callum

already he was conscious of his naivety
so many things that made him seem so green out there
any mistake or miscalculation
if he could hide it he would take the opportunity
an embarrassing kind of dishonesty he felt keenly
holding another full cup in hand
Arthur returned soon to Callum

a young man working away briskly
happily with Arthur's new toys
rolling the new machines backwards
down a stiff alloy ramp also new
the two men were soon standing beside the upright motorbikes
Arthur brushing fine dust
from the seat of one

sparkling new as they were
just travelled a few hours from Broken Hill
last section up the river road in a swirl of dust and dry air
he tried to calculate how many years it had been
since he straddled a bike of any kind
fifteen maybe
the height of the things surprised him

they're beauties all right Callum but thumpers
his friend laughed
you might be on your tippy-toes for a while
but you need something with a bit of reach out here
like we said the other night
you need a bit of fuel on board
just to ride the fence lines

don't want to be caught short out here if you can help it
Arthur quietly agreed *true true*
and the ute looks good too eh affirmed Callum
yep that's my idea of shopping all right
the bikes trailer ute and the drums and fuel
plus straps and stuff they threw in
all up you've still got some change out of seventy grand

not that you'll feel that ye rich bastard
Callum smiled and Arthur laughed aloud
suppose a bloke had better go and get his licence then
having all this stuff and all
Callum shook his head again
come on
I'll have a quick drink and then let's take these beauties for a spin

you can sort out the food and stuff later
I just dumped it all in the coolroom
as his friend moved away towards the quarters
Arthur walked around the new white four-wheel drive ute
the empty silver trailer
like the bikes they too seemed bigger
higher than he had imagined

and they certainly did not feel like his possessions
he chose the bike nearest to him
swung his leg up over the high seat
his weight pushing the stiff shock absorbers down
enough for the toes of boots to just touch the ground
look at you
lord of all you survey shouted Callum as he returned

Arthur sat quietly
looking ahead at the new vehicles
across to the trees
around the homestead
the river with its rough ribbon of green further away
weird he thought
a little while before

just down there
almost panicking to find my way
it all seems so logical
from here now
the lie of the land
or at least
one tiny corner of it

astride his new bike
wondered where they might now go
so many things to see
try to understand
within his 150,000 acres
perhaps head out along a boundary fence line
or cut across to the shearing shed to properly look around there

Callum pulled two new helmets from their packaging
handed him one
explained the bike's electrics
Arthur asked about the kick-start missing
discussed where they should go
given the time of day
Callum mentioned Harry might be there soon to lend a hand

it was then that Arthur remembered
the carvings
shocked
that for even a brief time
they had left his mind
before we do anything
there's something you need to see

Callum was less than amused
Arthur's hurried description
his attempts to drain the reservoir
the noise of the bikes suddenly ceasing
as they stopped at the base of the track
further sharpened
by the quiet of the warm afternoon

bikes eventually stood
near the moist mess of broken pipe and rubble
at the base of the broken dam wall
jesus Arthur
I made it pretty clear I thought
you'd be a mug to try that on your own
bloody lucky that's all I can say

Callum asked no more of what he was being led to see
angered by Arthur's impatience
worried what other advice out here
in country so new to him
would be ignored just as he pleased
Arthur felt bad about the whole mess
glad not to have to use words to explain

he'd only have to endure Callum's silence for a while
the sight of his find would surely change everything
as it had done for him
and so the two men arrived atop the twin boulder wall
looked down to the tight trapped chain
disappearing into a mess of a pile below
a tangle of stinking twisted debris

Callum inspected it all but without surprise
as if this was as he expected to find
he looked quizzically at his friend
Arthur pointed the way across to the other side
and upstream to where they could better see the inner walls
as they walked the path that already seemed familiar to him
Arthur wanted badly to describe what was there

prepare Callum for what he was about to see
but he found no words
instead
soon simply found himself standing on some still moist sludge
rotting branches amid his boot marks of the day before
waving his anxious hands towards the concave walls
both sides as if to guide Callum's impatient eyes

Callum drank it all in silently
then he spoke
quietly in a half moan
my lord look at this
Jesus Mary
this is full on Arthur
look at them all

Arthur felt a strange hurt
just looking upon the carvings again
yet being there to witness them a second time
seeing them there in that same place
the roo and emu
arcing parallel lines
marks he did not understand

seeing them there again
and with Callum there too as witness
made it all so much more real
a fact now
sadly true and right before them
two men walked along the filthy blocked creek
slime and rotting carcasses

straining to scan all that they could possibly see
numerous animals recognisable
plus a range of markings to them abstract things
clambered beside each other without speaking
occasionally exchanging perplexed and silent stares
Arthur retreated finally
moving back to the beginning of the path from which they had come

he let Callum break the silence
once finally emerged
man oh man
that is something else again
they are awesome
yet in here
drowned in all this muck

yeah Arthur concurred
feeling somehow calmer
his discovery now a thing shared
a heavy thing shared
it rattled me a bit
yesterday
you could say

well hell
I'm not surprised Callum reassured
it'd blow anyone away
there's just so much
and how many more we maybe can't even see
beneath all this slime and crap
a good thing Harry's heading this way

they simply continued to stare
until Arthur asked his friend
without a sense there would be an answer
how old would it all be do ye reckon eh
Callum looked different somehow
perplexed yet strangely enlivened by the whole thing
there's a question right enough

he pushed his thick dark hair back through both hands
held them behind his swirling head
slowly turning away from the rocky shadow formations
then back again
I don't know
I really don't
but Mutawindji may be a clue

it's a really special place
west from here
between here and Broken Hill
carvings there thirty thousand years old they reckon
but who knows
these things
well they weren't done yesterday

Arthur followed Callum back down the rough narrow path
negotiating the slim track in the speckled shade
heat of the afternoon gave them reason enough not to speak
at the base of the broken dam wall Arthur waited
Callum looked at the rusted pipe
pieces of rock
broken cement

he smiled across at Arthur
you did a right job of this eh
and both laughed at the sudden mess and tangle
the result of his impatient work
Arthur thought back on his folly
diving in there
the smell of stale water he still sensed on his skin and in his hair

yeah it probably won't be the last dumb thing I do either
just to warn you
Callum laughing until reading the cement marking
J.M. 1954 he moved closer and read aloud
repeated as if chastising
well J.M. whoever you are
just what were you thinking in nineteen bloody fifty four

4

Arthur struggled at times to keep pace with Callum
his friend not racing him or showing off
but wanted to stretch out
blow some cobwebs away
from the dam they had decided to simply ride east
along the southern boundary fence line
just to see what they could see

beyond the almost hills
fingerings of dry creeks near the homestead
it was soon all open country
a track hugging the fence well worn
Arthur followed the dusty trail of Callum always ahead
pulling up finally at a gate
a slight dog-leg in the otherwise perfectly straight fence line

three mulga trees offered some shade
they sat on silent bikes
dry sheep droppings sprinkling well worn ground
beneath the shelter of the tree
how did you go in those drifts of sand
Callum asked the less able rider
one section nearly caught me

I took it pretty easy to be honest Arthur replied
been so long since I was on a bike
any kind of bike
Callum was keen to encourage him
you go okay though
you'll be fine
it's so easy to go full tilt out here but a bit ugly when it goes bad

no shame in going slow
that's for sure
speed
Arthur figured he and Callum had different interpretations
he smiled at his friend
inspecting the state of the steel gate
then gazing along the whole fence line

they had ridden for about twenty minutes
Arthur had no concept of what distance that might mean
there was a bend on the map he recalled
about halfway along that south boundary
so he guessed that they were there
the fence is okay so far mate
not sure about up along there though

looks like it disappears a bit eh
Callum scanned the frail-looking line
stretching out straight ahead then all around them
whole place has been flogged though
not a pretty sight in parts
a shame because there's a lot of good flood-out country among it
some good loamy soils but there you go

people reckon they can just pack it full of stock
it'll somehow be okay
Callum spoke without expecting a reply
returned to the bike
ready to go again
how about we try to get up to the far corner
that'll do today eh

Arthur agreed and they were gone again
slightly undulating at times the track kept right along the fence
rough stands of stunted trees here and there
saltbush scattered
then thick for a while
the majority of the run was flat
tracks almost smooth

at what they presumed was the corner point
Callum stopped and waited for his careful friend
leaving engines running
motioned somehow that yes this was the corner boundary
their end point for the day
one end point of Arthur's realm
and so began the return ride

the vastness of it all
for Arthur both a frightening and an enthralling thing
dozens of straggling sheep
their coats thick and ochre pink
dotted the way
only the dry carcasses of some had he noticed
on the outward journey

wondered how many stock remained
missed in that last muster some months before
the last wanderers
escaping one fate for another
Callum had ventured a little from the slim path
Arthur followed
though even more wary on the uneven often rocky ground

they slowed to inspect a long water trough
at the base of a silent windmill
water low
but it was at least there
rejoining the fence track
they headed straight back home
Arthur standing more confidently on the pegs

he attempted to enjoy the ride
the feeling of speed and total freedom to move
while at the same time take in all he saw
though at the back of his mind always
the question of those carvings just seen
he was glad that Callum had mentioned Harry
he would feel better once Harry was there

as well as boxes of groceries and a cooler full of meat
Callum had also brought that day a carton of beer
on the wagon still are we Arthur
he asked hopefully
Arthur smirked at his own lack of will as he replied
yes and no
and today is no

accepting a partially cold can of beer
at which the two men gave cheers
quite a day Arthur
quite a day
Arthur fiddled with the fire as he spoke
becoming quiet
until it was a solid drawing blaze

they drank beers and fried some steak
speaking of the ways the property could be beautiful again
fences
feral animals
light stocking
cell grazing
and employment for a few

Callum began thinking of some names
wise heads to give advice
and some young fellas who really need work
something good to get their teeth into
they decided to also buy some camping gear
so they could ride the boundaries properly
in a couple of unhurried days

Arthur's licences for car bike and guns
they would pick off one at a time
would have to go over to the Hill
a fair bit at first probably
but then Arthur could do as he pleased
Callum was back at work after Easter
so they had that target and those few weeks only

an urgency around launching the thing
all positive plans
all things just there to do
all ideas fuelled by a campfire and beers
the great unsaid all that was contained up in that old reservoir
a tiny damp rocky pocket of history shameful
within the vast piece of land called Leopardwood

both men held the images in their mind
both put their hopes on Harry
Harry would guide the way
they slept deeply
in the lonely single rooms of the shearers' quarters
awoke in warm sleeping bags
to the early chill dusty sweet air

already mid-morning by the time breakfast fire built
then somewhat quelled
a full kitchen with power and running tank water right there
yet Arthur was enjoying the rituals that came with making the fire
with a familiar dull head from too much beer
he rolled a cigarette to have with his hot sweet tea
his lack of willpower made him smile and scowl once more

the clanking of a vehicle could be heard coming up the long dirt road
Harry waved his large beige stockman's hat out the window
slowing swiftly to a dusty stop
pretty early big fella
did you wet the bed
Callum walked over to the power company ute
to shake the hand of his old friend

naa
at least not this morning I didn't
I like to get up and away
and I couldn't wait any longer to see your beautiful mug
Harry laughed in a high-pitched giggle that was so unexpected
emerging from his bulky frame
he reached his hand out also to Arthur

good to see ye again Arthur
how ye settling in
Arthur gripped the large hand of Harry
hanging on through the handshake he had experienced before
yeah good good
one day at a time
he smiled and felt himself sigh

you'd better come and have a cuppa Harry
began Callum
we um
need your help with something straight away
Harry laughed
bloody hell
I'm hardly even out of the car

but then he saw the two men tense
exchanging serious stares
what is it
what's the go
a quiet moment before Callum almost blurted the news
carvings Harry
a whole mass of them

in the rocks here you mean
from the old people you mean
he seemed immediately both anxious and excited
yep and it's full on Callum attempted to explain
Arthur found them
after he busted open a big old dam
up the back of the gully there

Harry who was always agile
always moving
steadied himself
then determined
well come on then
stuff that cuppa let's go
I'll get me bike off the ute and we'll go

it was a deep faint sigh that finally emerged from Harry's barrel chest
his worn hat in both hands
held across the tight belly slightly bulging
oh my
oh my oh my
he spoke softly
squatting down on his haunches to gaze at the ground

Callum and Arthur looked at each other briefly
both judging that it was no time to speak
they watched Harry as he scratched at the ground
anxiously observing him as he tried to come to terms with what he saw
after gazing silently
breathless for a time
he had moved closer to the slimy wall

placing a hand near a group of markings parallel
walked off a little distance away
recoiling at the sludge and the grime
dark brown mud smeared down the side of his jeans
he remained there
scratching with a short blunt stick
at the dry soft orange sand

unusually nervous
after some time
Callum decided to pierce the silence
Arthur was wondering how old they might be
the almost always positive and jolly Harry snarled a weighty reply
how old
Jesus how old are the rocks and the sky

wouldn't matter
if they were fifty
sixty thousand years
or done maybe back when
back in seventeen friggin' eighty eight
they sure as hell didn't mean much to someone
someone back in nineteen fifty four

5

returning later that afternoon
Harry was in a calmer mood
though clearly thought Callum
his friend was a changed man
where's me dinner ya layabouts he boomed
marching into the dusty courtyard
ye haven't even got the fire going for a bloke

his light-heartedness a kind of gift
a signal to the other men that he was on the mend
the earlier anger he hoped they knew
not aimed particularly at them
well as a matter of fact you grumpy old bugger
I got a stew half cooked in there
and Arthur over the back chopping some more wood for the night

so any more questions or complaints
you can go straight to the manager
shut up and have a beer
Harry caught the cold can Callum threw
grateful for the drink and his friend's good humour
grabbed his coat from the ute
sat down on the timber bench seat in front of the cold fire drum

Harry drank deeply from the can
set it down in the dirt
pushing his hands down in coat pockets against the cooling breeze
Callum shouted from the open kitchen door
sorry squire but the maid has not yet set the fire
Harry laughed briefly at his friend's dig
but he didn't move

he sat gazing at the cold grey ashes
trying to sift through all the stuff of the day
despite the chill he felt with a quickening wind
he reached down for his can and drank some more
what an afternoon it had been
Harry had looked forward to the day or so out there
catching up with his old friend Callum and this new one

getting to know Arthur and the yarn behind him
he had imagined going for some lengthy ride on the bikes
pointing stuff out to Arthur
who seemed like a nice enough bloke
even if he was a bit quiet
Harry had even thrown his guns in behind his seat
to possibly knock over a roo

instead he had spent the day by himself mostly
walking up along a thin dry creek bed
among the memories and the etchings of his people
those who had walked before him
after the initial shock of the sombre long-drowned display
vaguely remembered Callum and Arthur
saying something about a ride

suspected they just sensed it
him wanting to wander there alone
they departed
once the sounds of the bikes died he walked
walked and wept as he walked
his back to the cavernous muck of the disgusting dam
some kind of desecrated grave

further upstream he walked
not expecting to find anything more
simply walk and keep walking away
without leaving the space entirely
the gully seemed to welcome him as it narrowed
beginnings of a breeze
perhaps the breath of the long dead commencing the journey home

his mind flipped back and forth
between the practicalities of notifying and documenting such a find
then feelings of anger and despair
damage that had been long ago done
walked through in his mind
a meeting with elders
both family and those known to him

visualised the line
those people so significant to him
his community
making their way
to that damp sad place within the gully dry
saw their faces long
heard their wails and cries

Harry even visualised a conversation with J.M.
after tracking him down
just to ask him why
but the ageing
weathered slender stockman of his imagination
just looked at him blankly before turning away
without need to explain such a thing from so long ago

just doing his job
working
making that hard country productive
what was this blackfella on about anyway
Harry saw again the face of his Aunty Grace
the soft dark face never far from his imaginings
sensed her tears as she spoke down to him in language

the greatest gift of the many she had given to him
language
the expression of culture
he murmured softly
recalling her words
almost her final words to him
almost her final words

a peculiar rattle tap
wood falling against wood
then the exaggerated laugh of Callum
broke into his thoughts and meanderings
I wondered how you would go Arthur
mixing wood chopping with drinking beer
probably not the ideal combination

so Callum shouted across from the kitchen
as Arthur gathered up the heavy small pieces
wood that had tumbled from his over-burdened arms
Harry smiled at him too
saying loud enough for Callum to hear inside
it's a bit rough don't ye reckon
when a fella gets criticised for having a go

Arthur tossed the short lengths down
onto the remains of last night's pile
behind the cold blackened drum
it blows me away how heavy some of this stuff is out here
Arthur said quietly to Harry
started to fiddle with paper and pieces of kindling
Harry long settled into his canvas camp chair

now leaning forward
as if anticipating the warmth of the fire to come
and some conversation
mulga is the heavy hard one
you've got a bit there in your hand look
that dark brown one
most of the rest of it looks like mallee

Arthur turned some of the heavier lengths in his hands
feeling the weight
exploring the different bark and the grains
it's a funny thing you know Harry
timber used to be my living once upon a time
I worked in a mill over near the coast for years
from when I was real young too

I know the stuff around there real well
logs we'd cut all the time
bluegum mostly
tallowwood and turpentine
always liked the stuff I did
I dunno
the smell of it and the feel

but you don't appreciate it after a while
like anything I guess
you just get so used to something
start to not see how cool it actually is
Harry nodded and smiled
yeah ain't that a fact
ain't that true

places too I reckon
I love this place
all this land all around here
all up and down the river
love it I do
but just the same
it's good to have people like you

new to the place ye know
bring it back to ye
it kind of sharpens your appreciation or something all over again
Arthur set down the lighter pieces
neatly in a small tepee form
around crumpled rough spheres of newspaper
the trick I suppose is hanging onto it

that sense of appreciation
to stay happy I mean
stay happy somewhere
Harry broke in
now you're in danger of getting a little deep old son
steady on
he giggled in his high chortle

happy
there's a thought
being happy
neither man spoke
Arthur took matches from his pocket
struck up the small blaze
quickly becoming their focus

flames took on a life of their own
Arthur soon added lengths of slightly larger fuel
there's one idea of happy right there I reckon
suggested Harry
nodding to the quickening fire
the late afternoon breeze was lifting some decent sparks
as it fanned the lengthening flames

I could sit by a fire all night
Arthur agreed
yeah it's good all right
warms the soul
then he smiled
and my old man used to say that when you cut the wood yourself
it warms you twice

Callum came out with a new beer for each man
returned to his cooking in the kitchen without speaking
what's this we get table service now out here
jeez I could get used to this
Harry winked at Arthur and grinned
Callum shouted back from the kitchen
I'm just trying to fuel you philosophers up

I've been listening
reckon that given time and a few more beers
one of you might even say something worth hearing
Harry and Arthur laughed
both standing to warm themselves closer by the fire
it was not yet cold
but there was an early autumn breeze and the sun was fading

the fire the place to be
Arthur surprised at how easy he felt speaking with Harry
given the events of the last few days
what about leopardwood Harry
how does that burn
Harry looked into the fire for a moment
then thoughtfully replied

well yeah
like most wood out here
it burns good I guess
so slow-growing and dense and all
but I don't recall just now using it especially on a fire
the sap is good for toothache
and the gum helps when little ones have the diarrhoea

explaining as a matter of fact
Arthur wondered how vast his knowledge of such things might be
and I certainly couldn't bring meself to cut one down
Harry concluded
why's that Arthur was intrigued
both by the actual conversation
and the fact that they were not speaking of the carvings

those carvings
that he presumed were troubling the minds of all
Harry keen to keep speaking now
it seemed Arthur was a fella who wanted to listen
and to learn
not just some blow-in with bucket loads of cash
flash money to throw around

well for one thing
they're just such lovely-looking things
stand out a bit out here I reckon
speckled
how would you say
mottled bark of greys and white
a kind of orange too

it does look like a leopard skin eh
kirinya is our word
Paarkintji word for 'em
but anyway
another thing
at this Arthur broke in
kirinya did you say

that's it
kirinya Harry replied
correcting slightly this fella he was liking more and more
maybe you should change the name of this place eh
Harry laughed
put up a big new sign out the front
Kirinya

let everyone know this is a Paarkintji place
they both laughed at this
but Arthur thought it was a fine idea
well why not eh
Leopardwood Kirinya under new management
Harry's high giggle dropped to a belly laugh at this
that's it that's the thing my brother

soon calm again
Harry continued seriously
in his steady explaining way
another thing I like about that old tree let me tell you
makes it a bit special to me
is the young ones
I'll show you some tomorrow if I can

them young ones
you wouldn't even pick it as the same tree
just a mass of spiny little branches
like some kind of nothing shrub
one of the shoots eventually becomes the leader
grows into this awesome straight trunk usually
not like most of the other trees around here

not like anything else anywhere I know
and some national parks fellas a while back were telling me
reckon that they evolved like that to stop all the megafauna
you know all those extinct giant dinosaurs
huge kangaroos and wombats and stuff
from eating them off
before they were mature

how good's that eh
clever bloody tree I say
Arthur was genuinely intrigued
pretty amazing he agreed as Harry enthused
I reckon it is
there's a lot we don't know
I've liked them even more since I heard that

everything around us you could say
is prehistoric
these rocks on the ground
them old lizards and snakes kicking around
Christ even the fuel in your brand-new flash motorbike eh
but I dunno it kind of gets to me that there
that little tree

here's this tree
clever little fella
growing in that same way
thousands and thousands
I dunno maybe millions of years before now
and it's still here
just doin' the same stuff

those poor old giant roos and stuff have long gone
but those trees are still here
doin' their thing
and guess what Arthur
I reckon they'll be here long after we've gone too
long after we here
enjoyed our last fire

Arthur was keen to learn more
yeah for sure they'll be here
does anyone know why all the megafauna disappeared
a mystery like all the dinosaurs
in reply Harry was serious at first
yep
there be a few theories around

meteor strikes and all that stuff maybe
but the best reason I've heard
I'll share with ye too eh
and he continued
through his engaging
infectious giggle
blackfellas

yep
it could've been us blackfellas who did 'em in
Arthur looked at him suspiciously
as if he were being set up for a joke somehow
but Harry kept laughing
assuring Arthur he was speaking the truth
no seriously bud

and you think about it too
Mungo Man was found not too far south of here
and what's him
about forty or fifty thousand years old
well some of those old giant wallabies they found about the same time
they would've been a big juicy feed I reckon
if you could knock one over eh

and none of them are still here
still kicking around
but here I am eh look
and with laughs he pinched at his well covered brown forearm
patted his tight round belly
yeah I'm like that old leopardwood tree me
still here and them gone

Callum emerged with a heavy black metal camp oven
pushed at the fire to make a bed of coals
strained a little to reach across the heat
to place it just where he wanted it to be
I'm still waiting
he said flatly
for one of you to say something worth listening to

yeah yeah okay professor
replied Harry in his calm baritone
I hope you've got some megafauna in that there pot
we're hungry ye know
amid the laughter of the other two Callum replied
yeah well big fella
you'll have to make do with some mega-lamb tonight

they drank beer and the talk moved to the ride
the state of the fences
erosion
signs of salinity
the stew would take a couple of hours
the wait was something to enjoy
the often silence and some conversation

taking turns
to push at the fire as they pleased
all thinking in their own way
of a crude dam that is no more
it was up to Harry to broach the subject of the carvings
and all that that entailed
and it took even him a while to get there

6

well
just when you think you've seen it all eh
the more Harry spoke the more Arthur admired his intellect and clarity
the discovery had affected each of them
though clearly Harry most of all
those rock carvings
the stuff of his ancestors

creations of his people
sat up there proud
for thousands of years
only to be immersed for the last few decades
sunk in captured water
covered in sludge and slime
disregarded disrespected

the three men sat
together for a long time that evening
by the fire
often quiet
amongst the spartan buildings
all whitefella things
things too likely built around 1954

Arthur did not know Harry well
not enough to detect any change in mood
yet he could pick up a sharpness
a quick precision
to his thoughts and words
a no-nonsense tone to his conversation
contrasted to otherwise jolly ways

incredible really
Arthur thought as he watched him
listening to their talk and often silence
that he wasn't in a full-on rage
fury at the white Australian world
this dominating culture
with the arrogance to flood antiquity

perhaps though
resilience had been a skill early learned
perhaps
mused Arthur
kicks in the guts
were things expected
swiftly recovered from

a beer-punctuated long conversation around the mulga fire
full of practicalities
hopeful future plans
spite and anger were in surprisingly short supply
though there was a sombre disappointment
at what had in years past
on Leopardwood clearly transpired

each man
with their so different backgrounds
came to the conversation in three complimentary ways
Callum the white kid
grown up just across the river
cleared out only to return now
a thoughtful and well travelled young man

Harry
the older of the three by not so many years
carried an energy and calm
came from walking confidently
in two such different worlds
and Arthur
the suddenly wealthy newcomer to that land

Arthur
in that country a still naive man
who had been flailing
in search of a life to spend well
sensed now
on Leopardwood
that he just might be getting there

their lives came together
among the lazy smoke and ruby campfire coals
each man sensed a challenge to their ideas
of what it meant to be alive
at that particular point in time
this place Harry offered
this place Leopardwood

Kirinya could become notorious
for what has happened here
like some places are
like the site of a known massacre
or something real bad ye know
'cause hey it was real bad
what J.M. and his mates did back in nineteen fifty four

it could be real easy
have people hate the place forever
who would blame them
just another classic example
though a bit more bloody obvious
more tangible than most
of the terrible things that happened

shabby old times
both then and still sometimes now
Callum and Arthur waited
through a few moments of expectant pause
hoping that he would continue
turn his thoughts around some more
Harry shifted the hot focus of the fire with the toe of his scuffed tan work boots

then spoke some more
or we could decide
that here is an opportunity
Callum and Arthur nodded
listened
here's a chance
make something good out of something so bad eh

I can just picture some of my mob
gunna hate it all
may never even feel they can come here
physically be here I mean
naa some of them will baulk at the gate
then some not even come at all
once they hear

full on
I don't think some of the old people could handle it
and some of the young ones well
Arthur
you better look out
I reckon some of those young fellas might wanta dust 'im up a bit
hey Callum

Harry laughed in his giggling way as Callum joined in
while Arthur
surrounded by the darkness of the cool night
his face a little drawn and unshaven
looked surprised and anxious in the fire's large glow
don't worry mate bellowed Harry
Uncle Harry here will save your skin

so to speak
more laughter
this time from all
naa they'll be all right in the end
Harry drank deeply from another beer
then continued
but fair enough they'll want someone to blame

you had nothing to do with it Arty
but you've gotta carry the can for it now I guess eh
Arthur let out a long audible sigh
Callum slapped him on the shoulder
smiling as Harry continued
more and more eager with his ideas
and so ye see this is why it's an opportunity

what's here
this terrible thing here
because it's so bad
and there's no one here directly to blame
we can't fix up what happened
we might not even be able to preserve what's left
god knows how damaged that rock is

what'll happen when it dries
who knows
it might all just crumble away
crack and fall
there would've been paintings up there too ye can bet
in them overhangs
all gone

how we learn
maybe even come together over this
well it seems to me that's the opportunity
you see
that there
crap like this has probably happened all over the country
so it has I reckon

but what d'ye do
crying's a good start
and I've done me share of that already
but how can we make something good out of it
it's too late to fix everything back the way it was
and I don't see you whitefellas
lookin' like you're gunna pack up and go anywhere soon

I don't reckon we've yet learnt
how to be together
we need to learn that
walk that walk
we need to learn how we can be together out here
and everywhere
everywhere

and crikey me
if we can do that here
well
people could do it just about anywhere I reckon
after a brief pause Arthur asked simply
you don't think I should give the place up Harry
to which the solid man replied

hell no
no bud I don't
no that's not gunna solve anything
what
give it over ye mean
Arthur leaned in to the fire
well yeah I mean it must be a special place obviously

shouldn't it be in the local people's hands
Harry smiled broadly at him and then turned to his old friend
almost shouting
Callum this fella is all right isn't he
of course ye just have to look at me to see you have good taste in friends
they all laughed again
Harry the loudest of all

it was a skill he had displayed throughout the evening
diffusing any sensitive tension with humour
usually at his own expense
followed by his high giggle guffaw
once emotions were checked
he would speak again
amid renewed calm

well ye see Arthur
that's all very nice of you and all
but let's not get too ahead of ourselves eh
I mean
first of all I've gotta notify the Land Council
that'll set off a whole string of visits and things but I dunno really
it's on a bit of a different scale for me

I mean
I've done a fair bit through the company
they often ask me
or another fella down Menindee way
to do their cultural surveys and the like
we try to check everything
to make sure

check there's nothing of significance
before a new power line or road
or something gets pushed through country
and we've seen stuff too
canoe trees and old middens
even a big tool-making area
out between the lakes down the way

but naa
nothing like this
not on this scale
not me
it'll be a big deal don't worry
and so it should be eh
National Parks and the museums

they'll all be here you'll see
but givin' it up Arthur
well
let's just wait and see eh
you've only just bought the place too
sighed the solid man
moving his gaze from the fire to Arthur

yeah but I dunno Harry
if I ever could feel that it was mine
all this
it might come with time I suppose
maybe with time
but I've never even owned a house before
let alone anything like this

even without finding those carvings there
it was going to take a bit to get me head around
Arthur felt the loose buzz effect of several slow beers
open now in a way that he wished he always was
without grog
he rolled a cigarette
another

committing once again to give up both
booze and tobacco sometime soon
Harry also by now well relaxed
it's a funny thing I reckon yeah
the idea of owning this here land
conversation may now go anywhere
any defences broken down by beer

Harry continued again seriously
I've got me own place over in the Hill
nothing flash
but I love that sense that it's my home
security I suppose is what that's all about
that there
but all this country here

just the idea of owning a big slab of country like this
I dunno
that's all a bit weird to me
I mean in the old days ye know
there was no such idea
we're all just custodians as they say
a responsibility but not a possession

but hey I've seen plenty of blokes
whitefellas too
who full on loved their bit of land large or small
you know
really wanted to care for it
make it more fertile
back like it would have been maybe

feel like they were improving something
not just making a quid from it
the three men sat among the vast black stillness
as Harry's thoughts hung in the air
you strike me Arthur
as a fella who actually wants to do some improving
could be wrong

but I reckon it'd be good for this place if you stay
Arthur nodded silently before Harry spoke some more
I mean there'll be a fair few people through here for a time
lots of people I'm guessing
apart from all the stuff to do with documenting and that there
may well be a whole bunch of our mob
wanting to come through here

Harry left a space for Arthur's reaction
the legal owner of Leopardwood struggled with a response for a time
then he ventured back into words
not clear at all what his tongue would say
yeah well of course
whatever you reckon needs to be
there'll um never be a padlock on the gate here

Harry was clearly well pleased
yeah I can see that Arthur
this new fella
Harry pondered
had the gift it seemed
able to listen
close his mouth and open his ears

combine that with his wealth and well
he might have an opportunity to do something good
what were you planning for the place Arthur
Harry pursued
I mean
just imagine for a sec that there was nothing but
sludge and slime you found inside that old dam yesterday

what would you be planning to do eh
Arthur shifted up a little in his chair
not clear of any detail he could give
well it needs a good rest if you ask me
the whole place
like Callum and I was saying yesterday
it's been pretty well flogged for a long time

I hadn't really got beyond the idea of fencing
there's a few months work in that alone I reckon
easily
but no stock for a while
christ there are still enough sheep and goats kicking around
enough we saw yesterday
despite the last muster they said they came in to do

I dunno
I've got this idea in me head of fixing it up real well you know
but I don't have a clear plan yet of how
Callum felt a need to put in
you need to get hold of a good manager
soon too I reckon
plus a team of fellas to get into that fencing

there's no way you or anyone can handle all this alone
you can't be tackling all this by yourself
you've got the money there
Callum broke off
worried he had been too open about Arthur's wealth
but Arthur straightaway
used the opportunity to clarify for all where he stood

these two men had his trust totally
not just because of the fire and beers
Arthur looked straight into the coals
though his words were intended for Harry
a few months back I came into some cash
Harry nodded and added as if a confession
yeah Callum mentioned the other day

something about a lottery win
Arthur smiled at Callum though not annoyed
it was a fact after all
yeah well he continued
seven million
bang just like that
rich

and I dunno
it's just there in the bank
even after some travelling and kicking around
buying this place and stuff
I was trying to work out yesterday
but I reckon
I'd be lucky to have spent a million yet

the other two men shook their heads
smiled to themselves and each other
hoping Arthur would continue now the subject had been broached
the dam breached
so I figure
if I've got this money
there must be something good I can do

I mean it's earning me more money all the time
just sitting there in the bank
that's the thing
Harry jumped in with his chuckle
just give me a call if it's burnin' a hole in your pocket won't ye
well it does in a way
Arthur quickly countered

never would have thought it
not in a million years
but it does come with responsibility
so it does
all this money and
I dunno
opportunity

Callum and Harry both poked at different sides of the expansive fire
rolling and folding the unburnt ends
longer pieces earlier set back into the glowing coal heart of the thing
quiet as they fiddled
giving Arthur time to place his thoughts clear before them
maybe it's because what I won so suddenly
just so much compared to where I was

I dunno how much Callum has told you Harry
but I was on the streets until just a few months ago
yep came Harry's acknowledgement
though Arthur was not demanding a reply
continuing in his quiet exploring way
speaking as if searching himself
looking in his words for what he really did mean

so where it would change the life of anyone
winning seven million quid
the average person you know
a mortgage maybe and family and whatever
for me it was like
man in the blink of an eye
I'm moving from nearly dead to the top of the tree

he paused to quickly drink some beer
that's messed with me head a bit
don't mind telling you
it still does eh
just have this huge
overwhelming sense
I have so much more with this gift of a second chance

had panic attacks almost for the first week or so
paranoid
sure someone was going to get it off me
that I didn't deserve it anyway
then this sense of guilt that I had all this stuff
and the poor sods who I dossed down with just a few nights before
still sleeping rough

out in the cold
or up at the Sally hostel queuing for a feed
then this whole sense of fear
scared that I'd waste it away
not use it to make anything really good come
that's when I decided to travel
bugger off for a bit

hoping I suppose
come to some grand realisation
about what the hell it was I was supposed to do
Harry looked across to him
wondering if there really was some kind of revelation that would come
and all that happened travelling
was I run into mugs like this

Arthur waved his half empty beer can
and most recently rolled cigarette towards Callum
as laughter came from all
and bloody lucky you did too
thank your stars Callum defended
more good fortune than winning that old lottery
meeting the likes of me

once the laughter had again eased
Arthur tried to re-thread his thoughts
Callum suggested I come out here
and I was keen too
never really been past the mountains before
then the next thing I know we're having a look at this place
it just kind of clicks with me somehow

I mean
if Callum had been somewhere up on the tablelands
or over near the coast and I'd visited there
might have been the same
but I dunno
I might have had the feeling
yep this is for me but I don't think so

reckon the interest for me out here is that it is so different
I have so much to learn
that might drive some people nuts
but I like it
good for me somehow
Harry stretched and moved closer to the fire
turning to warm his back

after a moment of thinking through the things just heard
he spoke again light-heartedly
it's different all right
first time I ever went over that way
over to the coast
a while back now
young fella I was

whole bus of us from here
headed for a footy tournament over Nambucca way
oooh Jesus I won't forget them hills
most of us had never seen that kind of country before eh
and anyway we get over to Armidale up on the tablelands
all that's okay but when we start heading down the mountains
some real steep places just pretty close to the coast there

man there was a whole bunch of us crouchin' down in our seats
real scared like
afraid we was true
Harry laughed as he continued nostalgically
old Peter I remember
big lump of man he is too Arthur
sitting down there right on the floor between the seats

scared he was
steep green valleys and towering trees
I reckon none of us looked out the windows for a while
laugh at it now but we must have been a sight
grown men scared of a few hills
but the beaches and rivers over there eh
and watching these fellas surfing the waves

now that's gotta be fun
did ye do that Arthur over there
Arthur smiled at Harry's enthusiasm
smiled with the memories of times and feelings so far away
yeah I've surfed I've surfed all right
it's wonderful all right true
Arthur's memory took him back to different days

not only back way back to the endless weekends and holidays
the beach of his adolescence
days as a young and healthy man
his memories were also far more recent things
bodysurfing in the early mornings
a clean wake-up
after a night of drunken rambling

bathing in underwear
all other possessions on the nearby sandy shore
energy just to float on in with the smaller broken waves
it was those mornings that highlighted for him his total fall
not so very many years before was he with friends
happy and strong with surfboards amid the waves
how quickly how effortlessly had it all changed

7

upon waking Arthur found both Callum and Harry at the fire
raking over the night before
there were cheers as he emerged from his room
bleary-eyed
yeah yeah I know
too much of a good thing
but as I recall I was not exactly alone

no I'm not a saint either me
offered Harry steadily
yet at least I know not to touch that there rum
that's the silly stuff
that's the stuff to make a good man bad
Arthur noticed the empty clear glass bottle on the ground
beside his seat from the night before

that would explain his worse than normal head
the stale sticky taste in his mouth
sheepishly he poured a mug of tea from the large pot made
skulked off again to his single stretcher bed
barely heard Callum and Harry talking and laughing some more
sounds of them trailing
as they walked off somewhere

god
you idiot
he cursed himself
climbed back into his companion of several months now
the feather-down sleeping bag
sat up to drink his hot sweet tea
lay back to feel his head swirl and stomach churn

reprimanded himself again for this hopeless failing
his history of too much booze
evenings that began so pleasantly
ending the next morning with sweats and the shakes
a blank mind searching back in vain
for the memory of several more hours lost
he had done this to himself

let himself do this
more times than he could count
a large part of his journey to the streets too
and once there it was almost an expectation
certainly replaced all ambition
but even since his reprise
it could still ambush him

since his unexpected financial shift
he had at times still
lost all sense and reason
to all manner of things within bottles
vessels of various shape and form
with the power to entice him
lure him to escape somehow

precisely what scared him now
even when he had the freedom to choose
decide exactly without sway
how he wished to spend each day
the stuff could still grab him
he would overindulge
leaving him to feel this hollow and familiar regretful way

from the stiff wire single stretcher bed
Arthur surveyed the imperfect narrow room
the still early morning light seeped through
framing the perimeter of the closed timber door beyond his feet
highlighting holes and tears of the window curtain above his head
ceiling white seemed quite recently painted
though with light dusty cobwebs aplenty

a bare solitary light globe hanging from its thick black cord
ceiling paint splotched somehow midway down carelessly
flecks on its brown bakelite
mustard walls a little chipped in places
totally bare if not for the noticeable flaking
light catching the pink-orange dust
hovering in corner cobwebs

something shifted on the floor
the faintest breath of moving air
a dead and dry feather-like carcass
brown spider
reduced to an impotent claw
blown across the hard surface as if a tumbleweed on ochre plains
spent spinifex dry dead cracked from its roots and tumbling

the bed squeaked as he moved in any way
narrow yet adequate
reminding him of the same in many a hostel room
hostels did not however offer the luxury of a single silent room
always crowded
if he were lucky enough to find a space
when he tried

he'd wake inevitably to the sounds of another man
too close and fiddling through a noisy plastic shopping bag
funny
thought Arthur
that he could be in a flash place overlooking the beach somewhere right now
waking up in a big fluffy soft bed with the morning sun streaming in
perhaps even without a rum hangover

crazy he had chosen to be there right now
the bed in which he lay
consequence of choices made
motorbikes started and soon trailed away
Callum and Harry heading off
perhaps down the river way
judging from the sounds diminishing

Arthur content a little longer right there
attempting more sleep in his shallow shame
slumber was soon visited by events recent and extreme
his shaky sleepy mind throwing up images from a past more recent
took some time for him to recall the face
somewhere contained in strange memory haze
her smiling face

that had not been smiling then when he'd stopped to help her
leaving his companions and the bottles in bags
to see why there was a new bundle of raggedy bones in his park
to see where they came from
who they belonged to
and he saw her face for the first time
beaten pale

it took some time for him to recall the face
through that bad memory haze of his
through those blurred hard nights of his
nights that were so long and sometimes broken
intervals of day and sleep
it took some time
for the face before him

her soft white
quite ordinary face
to loom any larger
than the thousands
troubled faces of stubble chins whisky-sticky
scarred and facing down
scarred and facing down to a not pretty ground

barely holding back the phlegm of last night's booze and rambling
from a not pretty ground
barely holding back the tears from the not sorry ground
it took some time for the face to rise out for him
it was smiling now
and he knew that brow
but he had not before seen the eyes nor that smile sincere

so at her he growled and turned right away
it was only when she spoke
of the other night and his kind help
and wouldn't he please accept this little token of her appreciation
as she tapped his hand that had made a fist
a fist clutching the sad lapels of his crazy-worn jacket
that was once warm tweed

she tapped the cream envelope on his knuckles tight
knuckles tight as if it really was cold and that jacket warm
and she said again
not smiling now
that she wanted to thank him
but didn't know how
she'd been left there beaten but getting better now

surely you remember
it was you who helped me
held me
brought me to that bench and lay me by the fire
went right the way over to the other side of the park
to get that cop you hated
but you brought him to me just the same

with his hand on gun
all the while probably thinking
you were setting him up for a beating
don't you remember
him taking over and you standing back looking shy
and then the ambulance
they took your coat from me

your coat that was warm
wrapped me in a blanket cold
tossing your warm thing on the damp night ground
don't you remember
slipping a glass flask of something into my stretcher
as you stood at the ambulance door
quiet and sad

they found that bottle too
but it was very kind
kind of you
don't you recall
I have a little something for you
just a little something
for you

fists released lapels
a head turned around to see her face
more familiar now as it frowned
not the unusual dream of a kind face so close to his own
a fist with knuckles white
evolved into an open palm of acceptance and trust
if a little blotchy and grey

a grateful cradle
for the simple gift of a neat white envelope
handed quietly to him
I remember
sure I do
sorry
said red puffy eyes

what's this then
ticket to paradise I suppose
at this the anxious young woman smiled
happiness gratitude and relief
perhaps came her thin voice
more fragile finally than that of her saviour's
her strange unfortunate saviour

now conscious and looking at her by glances in the eye
I hope so
you are a very kind man
she didn't weep
as she was sure she would
finding him and actually completing the task of thanks before her
and words didn't totally fail her

as she looked again into those moist eyes
those eyes that carried the hint of a shabby smile
he watched her trying to hurry away
he noticed the limp
saw again that dark and bloodied knee
she walked away from him without turning
he watched her becoming small across the park

it was early still
few pedestrians or cars
a young man put his arm around her
embraced her for a moment
before opening the door of a sleek new car
and she was gone
back into a world more familiar

Arthur sat up on his bench
headache looming as he rose
thinking of that young woman
that crazy night almost forgotten
just one crazy blurry night of many
and what's this thing then
this thing in my hand

his thoughts turning with the small object before him
funny some people are
a beating's a thing I try to forget
yet here's this one coming back
reminding herself of a bad thing
funny some people
coming back to the place of a bad thing

he looked at the envelope
smelt its cleanness
looked at it again
his hands
always grimy hands
filthier than ever against the whiteness of the thing
some smudges on it already

bugger it
such a nice thing
he turned it over again
read slowly on the front
to a kind man
with heartfelt thanks
S

the S made him smile
a signature but one without a trace
something you'd write as a mystery to someone
a puzzle to be solved
or maybe something you'd sign because there was some fear
fearing recognition but still wishing to leave a mark
you opted for the initial

almost anonymous
elegantly simple
with no hope of further contact
Arthur smiled at some possibilities
Sarah Sam Susan Suzanne
Suzannah Sonya Sylvia Sarojini
Sally Sal She Shim Salome

he smiled and opened the slightly smudged cream and lovely thing
expecting some kind of pretty thank you card
but there was no card as such
nor a letter thanking
applauding the fine deed done
perhaps he thought
she was not confident that he could read

but he did find and read
two very fine things that were there
the delicate paper of a receipt book
enfolding a square stiff card
fine paper told of accommodation paid
seven days at the Plaza Hotel
one suite room paid

the ticket it enclosed
a kind of funny extra lottery ticket good luck thing
millions of dollars to never win
but this is a receipt
this lady wants me
has given me
a room above the beach for a week

luxury and comfort
her clumsy lovely clumsy form of thanks
a hell of a thing for someone to do
another example of how weird people are
what a dumb stupid thing
and he wept
quiet tears of a face lonely

tears that well in eyes often red
finally traverse the face beaten
Arthur woke
his eyes moist from the deep sleep and the memories it contained
bikes returned and were quickly silent
he heard Callum and Harry speaking
couldn't catch their words

sat up on the stiff single bed
swung his feet down to the cold cement floor
bare feet slipping a little as he stood
the fine pink dust film seemed to permeate everywhere
no sooner had he stood and stretched
feeling slightly better in his hung-over state
did the bikes start again and his friends were once more gone

the remains of his mug of tea cold and sweet
sat down again to get into trusty boots
walking would surely help
his head was definitely not fit for the bike
mid-morning and once more a sharp clear day
not a breath of wind as he ventured outside
the heat not yet taking hold

two square-tailed kites swung above in their endless ellipses
ever watchful
tracing a broad arc
encompassing the scattering of structures man-made
crows and some other smaller birds
made a fuss about something over by the main house
so he decided to head that way

as he stepped across the soft dusty ground
recalled his solitary walk of a few months before
his slow walk from the park to the Plaza Hotel
meandered
as he did now amid all this new space
endless veins of dirt paths
across saltbush plains

he meandered then from the park
with the knowledge delicious
at the end of his walking on that day
there would be a hot shower and a soft bed warm
he walked through the park to the place he liked best
out along up high to the black rock ledge
a favoured quiet place

the park a fine thing
spreading up
rising up from the sweep of sandy beach
a steep gully of garden beds
clean pathways and lawns manicured
walked slowly through the city's patch of green
set aside for all by some people of vision a century or so before

his path derelict in the light breezy sun
beyond the well-tended calm of formal gardens
a place where you didn't sleep
too many tourists and picnickers there
and so the police
some gentle and others blunt
always keen to move you on

he moved up onto the mostly bare headland
to where he often did like to go
to stand facing the sea and breeze
look down upon rocks and an open sea
and that pool carved from a black rock ledge
carved by sorry convict hands
so the story was told

created for the settlement's governor long ago
with his presumably soft hands
could be bathed
Arthur stood there simply in the breeze
in the gentle salt air
with the weight slowly rising from his shoulders
shoulders long knotted hard

he stood with his back to those grey years of his
his back turned from a whole continent of strange sad problems
in time he moved again
roaming the scrubby goat tracks people had made
pushing beyond the barriers of where they were supposed to tread
high above his favoured rock pool
in a salt breeze on a pigface covered headland

he walked the afternoon away
stopping sometimes when his body began to groan and complain
sweating alcohol again
he stopped and smelt a cliff face breeze
no suicides today on that breeze
not today
not me anyway

the envelope secured in coat breast pocket
checked again
the walk resumed
at a slightly protruding overhang
by a graffitied urine-damp ruin
a cement pillbox
from a war that nearly came

he could look down upon the city beach
the origin of the afternoon shadows
the plain squat but glorious
Plaza Hotel
he could be there by now he knew
savouring the thought of a hot tub
suds and a colour TV

he pictured himself reclining
above the afternoon waves by the light comfort hum of a minibar
tapped the envelope once more
taking the road down through the park
that park of colour
passed his definitely favourite rock pool place
along the esplanade to the front of his hotel

gazing at the clean glass doors reflecting the sea and he
his bedraggled glory
he imagined the questioning look
someone clean at the front counter would surely question
and the porter with no task but to open a door to a room with a view
no luggage and no tip to wait for
Arthur smiled at the whole idea and walked away to a rock pool close by

there he washed a stubble face
pulled back some long hair
some nearly matting hair
with wet finger combs
before checking again the little envelope treasure
in his coat breast pocket
and he was on his way

the young woman at the front desk was quite a surprise
all crisp blazer and buttons gold
fresh-faced with shiny bobbed hair
Arthur anchored treasured worn boots in thick carpet burgundy
waiting for his turn and for courage
watching her swift movements
pens and phones and appropriate pieces of paper

the passage of credit cards
and the passing of bulky clunky keys
he stood back against a mirrored wall
back away from the desk and her
she dealt with a tall slender woman and a rather squat man
both in suits and barely responsive to her smile
talking to each other in staccato

signing things before them hastily with their one briefcase-free hand
the courteous young woman in a blazer navy blue
issued receipts and sincere business thanks
automatic doors released them
another busy suited pair
she stole a glance at the figure standing back
at the figure with no one left to stand behind

as he took a nervous step towards her
she offered the normal
may I help you sir
but she also took a little breath
and turned her fresh face around
in the hope that her workmate would return soon
to help with this street thing

once the treacherous burgundy carpet sea had been partly traversed
Arthur drew the envelope from his jacket
still quite white and clean thought he
looking shy and feeling flushed and awkward
just some little bruises of browny-grey on each corner
and this lady this lovely young woman
wondering what the hell is this guy up to

but I do like the way she's not looking at my clothes
my whole state of affairs
I do like the way her gaze stops with my face
my sorry face
he stepped up to her high polished oak counter
her polished cheeks
wondering what he could possibly say

she looked at his creamy parcel
held up as if an ornament by two stained and shaky hands
she looked back to those misty sad eyes that finally said
I recently received this
he passed the envelope
his treasure
to her

she opened it with care
unfolding the receipt
ah yes
we have been expecting you sir
then from her came a relieved faint faint sigh
the selection of appropriate pieces of paper
would you mind please sir registering here

and a pause
as she passed a fine pen to the grim foreign hand
all meals and in-house expenses for the week
have been taken care of
you need only sign
Arthur took the pen
with care not to touch her hand

he took the pen and looked away from the face
the face of the very lovely woman before him
who was treating him like some kind of human being
with tolerance and grace
he signed his name
as he pushed the piece of card and pen back across high polished wood
he for the first time looked her straight in the eye

attempted a smile
imagining the questions in her mind
she looked down and around for the large chunky key
pretending he didn't smell
smell like piss and the park bench he must have come from
wondering what he could have done
to be able to stay in a room she couldn't afford

a key was placed on the counter
together with his small envelope she returned
room 701 on the seventh floor
dinner is from six and breakfast until ten
both in the Dolphin Room
elevator just up these stairs
please enjoy your stay

Arthur blushed at her smile
looked down
her brass badge on blazer lapel engraved
grasping his key
he gave his silent thanks
Beth
from Beth this key I do accept

8

Arthur wondered what Beth would have made of this
his choice of home
silent but for the excited birds
a hawk of some kind he had not seen before
two of the square-tailed kites
swooped at something as he neared the outer garden fence back gate
roses lined the perimeter

some dead
others bushing wild
apart from this rough line there was no garden at all
nothing remained of a lawn he presumed had at one time been there
a space of twenty yards or so
between the veranda edge all around and the struggle of old roses
pink dust and small sharp stones

on the soft and deeper patches of sand
a series of casual arcs went as far as the stone path
then steps that linked the main house to the old
kitchen and quarters at the rear
arcs the impressions perhaps of a snake escaping
plenty of gaps and options for a snake to go between
stone blocks and soft dry soil

excited birds disappeared as Arthur approached
he could see no snake
but had convinced himself
alone there beside unloved roses
beneath the wide pale blue sky
a deadly giant of a venomous thing did somewhere lurk nearby
the idea of it becoming real

not a feeling he enjoyed
wondered why he was not on the balcony of the Plaza Hotel
already a warm mid-morning
into which he had awoken for the second time
by the time he reached the homestead garden
just a few hundred metres away
Arthur was a parched sweating thing

flickers of his dream still trailed behind him
the kind but distressed face of his accidental benefactress
forever perhaps only known to him as S
then Beth at the Plaza Hotel
the lovely Beth
Arthur stood in the warm sun
gazing at the dirt

the stone path
the elegant sweep of the deep veranda roofline
gazed up with his mind elsewhere
what would Beth think
his purchase out there alone
his travels she understood
but what would she make of this grasp at settling somewhere

he wanted to walk up the steps
take another look at the house
the so empty house
but remembered the snake
his body automatically recoiled
stepped backwards across the dry dirt that was perhaps once lawn
deciding to mount the veranda from the grander central front steps

a brief flurry of wind made him wince against it and the sun
sandy soil stirred and lifted into eyes
in a moment it was gone
the warm vast hush of the morning returned
five steps of stone
beginning wide and narrowing with each
curved gracefully up from the dusty base to the loose timber floorboard crown

Arthur noticed a garden water tap
in the shade of the stone structure just to the side
the metal pipe askew from the perpendicular
somehow free of its once firm moorings of sandstone
it turned easily for him
the water that slowly flowed a rusty dribble
close in colour to the earth that drank it quickly down

water that had no doubt begun in that 1954 reservoir
water from a metal pipe corroding for months or years
flowed out good for nothing
to a grateful dusty garden floor
Arthur at first turned it off but then decided to let it flow
drain away the remaining drops
from that putrid reservoir and all that it contained

whatever was left in that metal pipe
so clumsily sheared off by he
with a boulder lifted
could surely not take long to seep to a full stop end
Arthur stepped up onto the veranda
thinking that he might actually enter
the house that could be made into his own

the rushed inspection before purchase
included a brief walk around
but at the time he chose not to go inside
it was the property that he had wanted
not the large empty homestead
in need of repair
it was the space not the structures that drew him there

yet that morning
feeling the immediate cool as he walked along the veranda shade
knowing he had some time alone until Callum and Harry returned
he felt drawn to have a good look around
the expansive front door he was not yet ready for
so he kept walking around
weathered yet still firm timber veranda boards

looking through windows without curtains
he came to the large room he recalled from his first glimpse weeks before
the only furniture he remembered seeing anywhere
in this room
an upright piano
moved slightly away adrift
at an angle from the wall

perhaps it was to be moved as well
then determined not worth it after all
the room with the piano led out to the tennis court side
posts were standing
upright and straight
though no nets to be seen anywhere
several weeds here and there all dead too in the dry

a heavy metal roller in the far corner
long motionless
smoothed handle resting against the high mesh fence
this had once been a pretty serious affair
the tape lines still seemed intact
though elevated in parts from the rough ants' nest gravel all around
wind at work over several years

in some parts raised tape cast a shadow
as it hovered above the silent court surface
elsewhere consumed by small drifts of fine clay sand
it took not much imagination
to picture Sunday afternoons of a different age
cool drinks and cakes
children running from the veranda onto lawn

young men attempting to play well
in the presence of young women
piano and associated songs and laughter
a background to the tonk and pat
the languorous tennis games
it may all have happened there
but not for a few years now

from the veranda
looking beyond the dust
his line of roses gone to wood
the land fell away slightly
towards the distant arc of red gums
hugging the river's curves
the river too so very dry

since his arrival he had heard people speak of a rise on its way
any day it seemed
yet no sign yet
Arthur still puzzled at how these things came to be
so dry and yet the promise of water coming suddenly
water to restore life would flow down
yet without any rain

the smallest breath of wind was cool in the shade of that deep veranda
though the homestead was barely higher than its surrounds
the vastness of the place
gave the sense that he was perched atop a mountain peak
a fine site for a home Arthur resolved
wondering how long it had taken to decide which particular single acre
among so many thousands to make into the house block

whatever necessities brought that decision about
Arthur totally concurred
the house
weary though it was
seemed also to belong there somehow
its local sandstone sweeping base and rusting corrugated-iron roofline
all a similar colour and profile to the ochre ground

the still new and tentative owner
decided to venture indoors
retracing the veranda boards to the top of the central steps
turned the large round brass and porcelain knob to the front door
all had been cleaned not so long before
in preparation for the settlement of his sudden purchase
for the new owner to come

yet there was still that fine film
dust accumulated on the worn and slightly loose handle
the long unopened deep brown-red timber door and frame
magnificent in their strength and simplicity
the mechanism functioned
to his surprise
in perfect silence

Arthur entered into a wide central hallway
bereft of furnishings of any kind
seemed more than large
closing the door behind him
he felt a different kind of quiet and stillness to that outside
each of the four doors leading from the hallway was wide open
allowing light to flow right through

he walked quite quickly straight down the centre
over the lightly dusted once polished floorboards
looking left and right through open doorways
still not inclined to explore every inch of this house that he owned
Leopardwood homestead was a simple square
six rooms joining the central hallway
at the rear ending in the veranda which had been partially enclosed

Arthur opened the back screen door slightly but then hesitated
the next few steps
would potentially take him above the home of the snake
as yet unseen
he instead just looked across to the separate little cottage behind
the older simpler
original house of mostly stone

turning and walking back up the expansive hall
he decided that though everything needed repainting
sanding and polishing again
it was generally very sound
a new roof was the first thing he supposed
yet he could not do that on his own
so much he could not do on his own

yet he imagined himself quite happily over time
scratching away at the place
perhaps make it again something of an elegant home
Arthur was not back to the front door
when he heard the scream of the bikes going
noise lessened and suddenly stopped
arriving back at the shearers' quarters

he had enjoyed his visit to the big house
was ready for it finally
liked the way the large solid door
closed silently and properly
behind him
even with a snake perhaps nearby
sensed he might feel there at home

when he returned to the courtyard of their camp
Harry and Callum were emerging from behind the rainwater tank
faces and heads dripping
with the cool clean water
that tank's full now Arthur
but you'll be stuffed when it goes dry
Callum cautioned

Arthur smiled at his friend's ability to coolly summarise
yeah and I was just over at the homestead too
you can almost see from here
those big old tanks at the back there are good for nothing at all
there was still some water in the pipes
leading down from the reservoir that I let go
putrid muck that it was

that'll be the last of that stuff then
Callum laughed
maybe you should've bottled it up eh
for posterity
before Harry intervened
a reminder of something bad don't you mean
stinking business

good on ye Arthur
get rid of the lot of it I say
how did the place over there look anyway
ready to move in eh
not exactly no Arthur smiled
though it was a bit better than I recalled
I've got a bad feeling that there's company underneath too

a bunch of birds were going crazy at the back there when I arrived
and tracks in the dust
look like a snake's to my untrained eye
to which Callum taunted
there you go Harry
there's a good job for you
he loves snakes does Harry here

yeah be stuffed if I do
replied the big man
you're on your own there Arthur
I'll visit when that snake's gone
promise
but not before
Harry looked visibly chilled at the thought of the thing

Arthur was surprised by this
Harry seemed so attuned to everything to do with the land
never occurred to him that he may have fears
prompted by Callum's laughter Harry continued
and who says this blackfella gotta like snakes eh
probably a king brown or a taipan too over there
nasty bloody things them

Callum laughed a little louder which Harry duly ignored
speaking to Arthur it seemed only
it's bad enough
when you come across them in the bush
no one likes that
but you just kind of deal with it
get around 'em somehow

but knowing they're there and going looking
well that just ain't natural
at least not to me anyhow
Arthur agreed and felt that he knew well the chill down the spine
so visible in Harry as he spoke
the problem it seemed
would be for a time unresolved

Arthur reprimanded himself for thinking that his new friend
his Paarkintji friend
would immediately turn snake wrangler upon his request
the problem was Arthur's and he would have to solve it
pure luck that Harry and Callum were there with him at all
the owner of Leopardwood he pondered
better get used to sorting out problems for himself

9

it's down here somewhere
on this bank Callum
I know it is
Harry had insisted that they return again
despite the first unsuccessful hit out that morning
while Arthur had earlier crept gingerly around his homestead
Harry and Callum had been in search of a particular tree

now all three stopped their bikes near the pump housing
silence again once engines cut
something almost unnerving
as they began to walk
Callum and Arthur followed a little behind Harry
clearly intent on finding that one important red gum
you'll tell us if you spot a snake won't you Harry Callum called

I'll do better than that ye smartarse
shouted back the big man
steaming on
wide-brimmed hat
creasing in his hand
I'll throw the mongrel back your way
greeted with peals of laughter

after a few hundred metres
wending their way along the loamy dry soil
high river bank
meandering between and around the huge river red gums
spaced apart as trees in a child's picture book forest
the trees' huge trunks well spaced
only sometimes an interlocking high canopy

leaving plenty of room for the small folk below
between gargantuan trunks and roots gnarly exposed
to wander and amuse themselves
Harry stopped
as he waited for his friends to catch up to him
turned around slowly
scanning the trunks of each living ancient thing

hoping he would soon be reunited
with that one canoe tree
a roo bounded away suddenly as Callum and Arthur approached
then another took off a little further away
this interruption soon gone
silence returned
dappled shade some relief from the midday sun

at the base of the steep and scoured dirt bank
the little remaining water
a lonely milky-green algae pool
the large log of a giant long ago succumbed
collapsed into the water
decaying bulk
once again revealed in the dry spell

it's been such a long time I guess
Callum offered
not confident that Harry would find the tree
wanting to say that he didn't expect him to
yeah true agreed Harry
but he would persist he knew
well over twenty years I guess,

but we came here a fair bit
a beaut spot for fish then
we could see it across from its twin on the other side
your brother and I as we fished
a kind of marker for our favourite spot see
a bit hard maybe looking for it from this side
though I reckon it's close

but then
maybe the pump was in a different spot too
this slow
outwards bend I seem to remember though
it was up the top of the bank like here
the tree wouldn't have been taken by a flood
not gone down yet I figure

then Harry made them jump a little
he spotted something
darted off a few yards further away from the bank's edge
look here look
look up 'ere you fellas
Callum and Arthur hurried to the tree
to see Harry with both hands pressed upon the lower trunk

gazing up in wonder at the large elliptical scar
staring
all were silent for a time
until Harry stepped back nearer to them
and wept a little as he sighed
so how about that eh you old tree
you old canoe tree

he laughed as well as cried
look at me the big bloody sook
and they all laughed a little
Callum slapping his friend on the back
as Harry excitedly continued
some stuff like this though from long before
it just makes you feel like those old people are right here

we get it Harry
we get it mate added Callum slowly
Arthur gazed at the thing before him
a symmetrical vertical ellipse
carved out of the large torso of the tree
bark had resealed the wound around its edges entirely
yet the cut had been deep

the scar easily a couple of inches
below the surface of the rest of the tree
I just can't believe the length of it
Arthur offered as his thoughts
expecting neither explanation nor reply
but Harry wanted to speak
to speak about this special thing right there before them

it's an old one all right
you think about when those fellas would've cut it all out
where we're standing now
maybe they had their fire over there that way
not too far away
dried it and smoked it and carried on
did all those things they wanted

tease it up into a little canoe
and for that there to happen
for that same scar to be here
sunken back into the tree now
well it's gotta take a bit of time
what do you think Callum
Mr Earth Sciences University man

two or three hundred years or so do ye think
Callum nodded
eucalyptus camaldulensis
a couple hundred I reckon easy
Arthur continued Harry suddenly
it's some place you have here
fragile too

one big flood
or some dope with a chainsaw
could see the end of this old fella here
our people need to see this thing
whitefellas too
so keep it safe here eh
ye get it though eh

Arthur smiled and nodded
thinking how hopeless
absurd the notion
now suddenly he the owner
custodian of anything there on that beautiful fragile land
simply because of the fate of sudden wealth
plus other good fortunes thus far

before he could answer his excited and proud local friend
a true part of that same place
Harry began to speak again
Uncle Cecil
we need to get Uncle Cecil out here
this tree he'll know about I reckon
but those markings

those carvings away up there
man
what is he going to make of that
it worries me
worried how any of the old people will handle it
seeing all those carvings
up in that stinking old dam

they stayed a little while at the tree
mostly not speaking
Callum walked away by himself as he often would
thoughts and concerns tumbling through his mind
Harry took photos of the canoe tree
every possible angle
using his mobile phone

a bit crazy isn't it eh Arthur he beamed
there's no reception out here and I know it
but I still carry this thing around
a good thing I did today though eh
I'll come back one day with a decent camera
or get someone I suppose
document it properly

Harry became a little more composed
then suddenly sad again
Arthur watched the big man turn off his phone
returning the shiny thing to his jeans front pocket
clear that Harry too
had things on his mind
matters to consider

Arthur moved away
back in the direction from which they had come
surprised when Harry began to speak again
those carvings up there are stressing me out something fierce
they need to be photographed properly
real quick I reckon
documented

just imagine how fragile they'll be
immersed for so long
even worse
would've been in water
then dry at times
soaked again
some years better than others

and now suddenly dry
especially the ones up high
anywhere direct sun
where sunlight might sneak through
have to crumble away you'd reckon eh
I dunno
it's crook that's all

at least we're heading into winter
not the summer sun
though even that might be a worry if it's a cold one this year
we get some wicked frosts out here don't worry
that might be worse than the sun
imagine all them little particles of water in the rock
expanding as it freezes

man that'd be worse maybe than the sun
Arthur left the next pause alone
sure that Harry would have more thoughts to articulate
sensing that he was somehow finding calm and comfort
verbally searching for the right thing to do
they walked silently together
then Callum caught them up

remind me Harry
who's Uncle Cecil again
Harry replied immediately
brightening a little as he spoke proudly of his family
me Nan's nephew
Uncle Cecil
worked on properties all over here when he was young and later too

not much he doesn't know about round here
need him to see this
and talk to you too Arthur
a few things we'll need to talk through
Harry broke off with his broad challenging grin
we might just boot ye off here yet
us Paarkintji mob

10

it was a kind of melancholy that descended
the evening Callum and Harry left him there alone
Arthur laughed at himself
chastising in his own silent way
but he could not make it go away
that strange mix of sadness and loneliness
tinged with not a little fear

all were emotions with which he was familiar
his time on the street plenty long enough
to plumb the depths of most emotions known
yet this fear was a new kind
as it was not the primal
survival variety
his usual companion while he lived on the edge

rather it was now more about the possibility of failure
and in so many ways
he remade the fire in the courtyard
before the long slow shadows of the afternoon
led to the quite sudden dark
instead of preparing a proper meal from the kitchen so well stocked
he started again to drink beer

chose a small packet of dry biscuits as a token meal
the fire soon a comfort
yet it also in a way highlighted his solitude
silence now before it
a stark contrast to the laughter and company of the night before
fear would sneak around him too
recent fortune made him feel in some way vulnerable

way he had heard it said
of the birth of a child
there was suddenly so much joy
yet with it also a huge sense of responsibility
instant wealth that came to him
just a few months before
introduced both possibilities and fear

so he had flailed around for a time
travelling
the thing procrastinators had done for years
meeting Callum in Japan
then visiting him out there as promised
ending with the impulse buy of Leopardwood
a purchase only possible for those with money

another new joy
yet the source of some new fears aplenty
then through Callum he had met Harry
two men whom he respected more and more
grew to trust them already
hated the thought of letting them down
wanted to prove his worth to them

yet the scale of the country
now responsible for
work involved in that
only beginning to sink in
when he drained that stupid old reservoir
exposing images
releasing some ghosts of the property's past

his goal unchanged
since that day
day he received a winning ticket
simply wanted after all
wanted to do something of real worth
wanted to sense
his life was worth something

so close had he come to nothingness
had lived nothingness
his time on the street and before
he feared failure
even more keenly
given the power of resources
now his

mostly he feared disappointing
especially people close to him
all new friends
yet loyalty he felt
an eagerness to please almost
the common denominator among them he pondered
perhaps their simple decency

as he fiddled once more with fire
a larger than necessary open fire
pondered their decent honesty
they knew of his wealth
his journey thus far
Callum and Harry
shared the knowledge of his finances

now his dilemma unfolding
all that Leopardwood
had exposed
people solid in themselves
or at least to Arthur seemed so
had simply accepted him
as he was

Beth
lovely Beth
knew nothing of his latest exploits
he had written to her several times
from places various
even beginning a diary for her
imagined he would one day present to her hands

yet Arthur had not seen Beth
not since the Plaza Hotel
so long ago
those few months before now seemed
he felt close to her too
in just a few days
loved her calm honesty

she had been after all
the first person to regard him as something human
even in their simple interactions
across a polished timber hotel desk
she looked him in the eye
on that first encounter
not at his clothes and grime

he could have jumped into a new car
chartered a plane
just to find her the very next day
that day might come he supposed
smiling wanly into the flames
flames gradually creating
a deep bed of hot coals

but on that day
he would much prefer
to have something to say
something that would explain
his contribution to the world
or at the very least the effort
that was in some way good

should contact her again soon though
he decided
before losing touch entirely
she would know nothing of his most recent news
only that he was heading back
back to Australia
deciding where to make himself a home

all he knew of Beth
was that she too was heading overseas
thanks to a farewell gift he had left for her
the day he ventured out of the Plaza Hotel
began the journey up to PNG
he wrote two cheques
one hundred thousand dollars each

one he sent to the Salvation Army
for always caring for folk like him
souls in some form of disrepair
always there
the other he left at the front desk
for Beth
to help her on her way

the Salvos donation made him feel good
though he wondered
should he not have given more
the gift to Beth
an idea he loved at the time
but since troubled
feared wrong of him somehow

he thought she was lovely
yet expected nothing in return
so beautiful he thought was she
way beyond the affections of he
not even meaning to impress her
with money in that way
just a simple thank you to someone open and sincere

Arthur felt that Beth would use every cent
utilise positively
a few letters exchanged
since the shock gift
enabling her to inhabit some dreams
letters he hoped allayed her fears of anything more
almost convincing himself that it was so

Arthur awoke with a chill
and a beer on the ground
the final can of the six-pack
earlier retrieved from the cool-room
fire still alive bright deep coals
blearily he figured
he must not have been asleep for so long

now disturbed
he longed for the simple stretcher bed
familiar warm sleeping bag
in his single man's shearers' quarters room
there were faint flashes of a dream
Beth in a dream
to which he hoped to return

his night was thus spent
in the total dark and silence
his small room
within the simple workers' compound
within 150,000 acres
land he now legally owned
his responsibiity

night alone in the vastness
an eerie expanse that the darkness obscured
sometimes accentuated
a restless affair that sleep
the disquieted sleep of the less than sober
so vividly each time he awoke
her face and the first few days of their acquaintance

so near and far seemed the Plaza Hotel
he dreamed and woke
dreamed and roused once more
saw himself move to the balcony window
mid-morning sun now sharp
warming surfers
bathers and those strolling on the boulevard below

it struck him that every person he could see
simply happy to be there
to be alive
true there may be demons
lurking in souls unseen
monkeys metaphorical riding on backs up high
yabbering nonsense about addictions unclear

he could not see
if anyone's happiness
was true
how is that ever possible anyway
yet it certainly seemed so
people choosing to walk in sunshine
or to play in a clear blue sea

Arthur let his eyes wander the simple beach scene
after a time he wished to join them
suddenly longed to be one of the ordinary souls
walking on the firm wet sand of low tide
picking up a nicely shaped shell
rolling it about in his hand
tossing it back down

walking on without purpose with trousers rolled
yet he could not join them
he could not yet see himself among them
just hours since his gift was received
the newsagent dumbstruck and pasty-faced
checking the ticket and announcing Arthur's improbable win
there was still no cash in his pocket

he was yet to touch wealth of any kind
even when he did
Arthur was unsure
could he ever sit with ease
at the table of the mainstream
his only comfort still
was the room

his hotel room
not large but for him so full of luxury
his huge window onto the world below
Arthur pushed the glass doors open wide
coaxing the faintest of breezes inside
faint but full of the sense of salt
full of freshness and potential

the phone rang loudly
shattering the calm
strange he thought that it should ring at all
and so unnecessarily loud in a room so small
annoying as it broke his thoughts
though his thoughts were characteristically unclear
Arthur was agitated

until he heard the voice of Beth
hello Mr Catchpole
yeah he flatly replied
this is Beth from the front desk
I've just started my shift and there's a message here
saying that you wished to see me
I hope that nothing is wrong

how can I help you
in one breath Arthur's heart sank and soared
struggling a little for logic and calm he offered
no no nothing wrong nothing wrong at all
a pause at the other end then
so everything is fine then
Mr Catchpole

Arthur paused a little before he struck on it
well as it happens
I've had some good news
some news that I may need some help with
funny he thought how the mind can work
how the tongue can explain so clearly
ideas that in his mind were in draft form still

when suddenly they burst forth
lucid and with purpose
expressed to the world
thus becoming thoughts concrete
Arthur waited for Beth's voice
some good news
that's wonderful

we would be only too happy
to assist
of course and um
would it be easier for you to come down here
rather than speak over the phone
anxious to conclude
Arthur demurred

yep sure that would be good
I'll be down soon
thank you
no problem
any time
I'll be here till this evening
bye now said Beth

thank you Beth
said a soft Arthur
looking forward to seeing one lovely face he could trust
he put on his jacket
feeling the inner pocket for his winning ticket
there safely housed
then checked himself in the mirror

as he had done more and more that week
that week in his room a new safe haven
with an increasingly familiar figure
looking back at him
Beth offered a half smile to this strange man
this man
who was beginning to intrigue

perhaps not as old as he first appeared
that street thing suddenly respectable
but a fragile thing still
unsure of himself and everyone
Arthur approached the high polished counter
not sure exactly what he was about to say
but trusting his tongue as he had before

he placed the lottery ticket on the counter's polished grain
he placed it there as a kind of simple prop
an assist to the drama he wished to unfold
a small new unlikely story he had to share
a very lucky thing happened to me today he began
well actually
last week I guess my luck really began

when a lovely lady
to whom I'd offered some help
wanted to repay me in some way
gave me this room for a week
in your very lovely hotel
Beth looked at his soft anxious face
then glanced a little puzzled at the ticket

before returning to the face that seemed to change
growing calmer before her eyes
as it found its way around its own words
well the thing is
my luck has continued
Arthur now picked up his prop
that same lady also left me this ticket

and this little ticket has brought me more luck
in fact a heap of luck you could say
at this Beth let out a funny kind of muffled cry
bringing a hand up to her face
belatedly masking her reaction
you've won the lottery she asked
seeking to confirm the obvious

and though she hated herself as soon as the words left her lips
how much exactly
Arthur surprised himself with his matter-of-fact reply
exactly seven million dollars
Beth blushed but he really did not mind
I'm so sorry
that was very rude

no business of mine at all how much
but
congratulations
and then
recalling his phone call
and so how can we be of help
Arthur was now feeling well pleased

he had articulated his winnings to someone
the thing somehow seemed real
well two things I guess for now
I would like to extend my stay
the end of my one-week gift I'd already begun
begun to dread
but now I may stay and stay and stay

certainly Mr Catchpole
you certainly may
said Beth resuming her work pose
that will of course be our pleasure
while thinking to herself in a flush of envy
seven million dollars
just imagine the freedom

the freedom that would bring
and she smiled and waited for news of that other thing
the other thing is that I will need to go to a bank
Arthur said softly
Beth again embarrassed herself with a laugh
yes I dare say you will
or maybe just start your own Mr Catchpole

Arthur smiled at this and then stressed
Arthur
please call me Arthur
thinking Arthur the millionaire
strangely
how odd to experience this weird material change
there was an almost confidence building inside him

based on nothing he had done
nothing achieved
simply an acknowledgement of wealth
suddenly it was he who had money
no doubt purely because of this
many people would suddenly think him worthy
perhaps Beth would be one

yet she would always be a cut above
as she had proved days before
while he was still dressed in rags
looking him in the eyes with
some kind of
simple warmth
humanity

many may see his money
therefore think him worthy
but certainly not he
Arthur had self-loathing to burn
it would take more than a long line of numbers
figures in his new bank account
to clear the slate with his conscience

he straight away knew
he would have to do something
felt already
some good deeds would need to flow
and so how can we help with the bank
queried Beth
well I don't know for sure

but I guess I'll need a witness
whenever I actually deposit it I mean
as it is such a large amount of money
but I don't know
I've not been to a bank for a while
not for the first time
Beth caught a flash of the street

the crumpled man of just a few days before
even that awful musky stench
urine smell that had accompanied him
to her counter
on that first day
returned as she looked up at his ticket-cradling hands
the heels of his hands resting on her counter

the simple ticket
had changed one life so much
some grime lingering beneath nails
the only betrayal of a life before
Beth considered a safe reply
not knowing what the bank would want
except his money

I'll speak to my manager
but I'm sure that will be fine
then her clear mind wanted more details
do you have an account anywhere
even as you say
you've not been to a bank for a while
Arthur had wondered the same

well yes
I was thinking of going back
to my old bank
though I have no old bank books or anything as such
I have kept an old driver's licence always
it's out of date
but I've had this thing

this thing about always having
some kind of identification
something on me at all times
if you get what I mean
and so he produced it
reaching deep into his stiff new jeans front pocket
a single plastic card

betraying the established cracks of time
in the bottom right corner
his small photograph
Beth smiled
reaching across for the worn object
and so who is this
this handsome young fellow

oh I know I know flushed Arthur
as a schoolboy elated
just someone I used to know
give me that thing
then he looked at his face
triggering a smirk from he too
then the jolt of other memories

the times he'd clutched that card thing
held on to it as some kind of lucky charm
following a scuffle or a drunken brawl
why had he not realised before
his licence was his only true possession
watch and wedding ring long ago pawned
he refused to lose his little tag of identity

somehow he had kept it safe
and now Beth had held it briefly
that too was a nice thing
retrieving it
he thought of future
finer protection
I need a wallet I guess

feeling another blush warm his face and neck
not expecting thoughts to emerge
but Beth saved him
her lightness again
well clearly
Mr Arthur Millionaire Catchpole
you do

awake on his single stretcher bed
faint shafts of morning light began to pervade the small room
Arthur rolled over
retrieving jeans from the floor where he had discarded them
several hours before
knew full well that it was there
but had to check it just the same

the smooth kangaroo-skin wallet
the cracking fragile licence
in its clear plastic frame
that thing of his
Beth had once held
that one token of identity
Beth had once held

11

Arthur's ute pulled up as he emerged from a hot morning shower
Callum climbed out from behind the wheel
spotting his friend walking from the shared shower block
across the dirt courtyard
toiletries pack in one hand
a damp white towel across his shoulder
you'd better go easy on the water mate

now you've stuffed up that beaut old reservoir
Callum grinned
a deep slow chortle emerged from the passenger side door
this Arthur presumed to be Harry
but an unfamiliar unshaven face instead emerged.
Arthur this is Sid and Sid this here's Arthur
introduced Callum as the two men moved closer to shake hands

Sid's the old friend of my Dad's I was telling you about Arthur
he worked on our place across the river for what
how many years
Sid was examining the youngish man he'd just heard so much about
this new and accidental millionaire
he glanced also at Callum to answer him
oh ten or so I guess

yeah ten or twelve years with your old man
across the river there
before that on some other blocks around here
never this one
though I remember someone talking about that old reservoir
the last place for water
once the dams and the river and the tanks were all dry

Callum tells me you've buggered it in your first few days eh
Arthur measured up this new man
quite short but bulky and broad
a rough firm handshake paw
the accidental millionaire felt at some kind of disadvantage
standing there in fresh clothes with his moist towel
Callum and Sid in their work clothes and boots

the ute was stacked with more stuff
tools Callum had determined Arthur would need
they had clearly already been busy the day before on his behalf
not to mention the several hours drive from Broken Hill that morning
Arthur furthermore presumed that Callum had explained much to Sid
about himself and his circumstances
yet he knew nothing of this new man

this older man suddenly there
Callum had the other night mentioned
a mate of his Dad's who would be ideal
a manager
Sid and he were not beginning on a level playing field
though Arthur figured if Callum thought he was a good man
then he must be

yeah well
if you are going to stuff something up
there's no point messing around
just launch right in there eh
Arthur took a punt on self-deprecation
the two men's swift laughter
proving him correct

it was a mess up there though
that water wasn't good for much I don't reckon he emphasised
and Callum tells me you had a bit of a surprise waiting for you too
Sid stood with both hands in the back pockets of his tight work jeans
the stance accentuating his tight protruding belly and barrel chest
waiting a few minutes for Arthur's reply
as Callum busied himself with the untying of the ute load

the carvings
well yeah
you could say I wasn't expecting them
no
Arthur looked towards Callum
sensed and expected
the surprised glare from his friend

I hope you don't mind Arthur
letting Sid know about all that
but it's a bit of an issue you've got up there
and this fella might help with organising your water somehow
Arthur nodded and half-smiled at them both
like so much it seemed
out of his hands

Callum further justified himself
and he'd find out before long anyway
it'll be a bit of a big deal around here once people know
prompting Sid to check
Harry's seen it you said
to the quick affirmation from both other men
well shut the gate then eh

it'd be across the grapevine by now
and that bush telegraph is a mighty fast thing
I'll tell you that for nothing said the decisive man
well welcome anyhow Sid
Arthur announced
keen to speak no more with someone he did not yet know
speak not of the thing most eating at his mind and heart

I'll just dump this towel and stuff and we'll have a cuppa eh
unload all this gear
looks like me butler over there has added a few more things
a few extras to the shopping list
as Arthur walked away to his single room
Callum replied louder
and your butler doesn't want to forever be the delivery man

we've got to get you over to the Hill to get your licence sorted
need one to get a gun licence too
to which Arthur shouted from the step up into the open door
and what do I need a gun for
Sid looked askance at Callum
as if to confirm what Arthur had said
could this fellow really be so naive

it took some seconds for Callum to compose an answer
well the thing is Arthur
there are a few reasons a gun is a good thing to have around
most farms have guns I reckon
like it or not
stock need to be put down sometimes you know
and out here well you don't have a vet within a few hours away

and then there's the ferals
you want to be picking off any pigs whenever you can
or they'll be getting on top of you
and if you want this place to look anything decent any time
well then they're something that need to go full stop
not to mention the odd snake in the wrong place
like that there king brown or whatever underneath your new palace across the way

you need a gun Arthur
Callum's simplistic and definite conclusion
enabled Arthur to smile and reply
well when you put it all like that
seems more like an instruction than a suggestion
but okay I get it
I'll get a gun

put it on the list
something else to learn
prompting Sid to offer
there's something I can help you with straight away
brought mine out with me
thought we might drop a couple of roos
maybe chase a boar

tonight eh
you'll get the hang of it
with Callum jumping in
learning how to be safe with the things is what you need
need to get that right
after that it's all just practice
like anything

okay then we'll see
what else is loading up that ute of mine then
asked Arthur
keen to move everything along
well began Callum again but more animated
I took the liberty of investing in a few tools for you
for the place

just stuff for some fencing
mattock and shovels and a bar
plus a fair collection of hand tools and whatnot
anywhere you look stuff needs doing
we might even make a start on that old homestead if you like
I've got two more weeks basically
before I start back at school

much of what was unloaded
placed in the breezeway near the kitchen
a new wheelbarrow the bulkiest item
the rest mostly new tools in their boxes
power tools of every description
an array of hand tools and nuts bolts and nails
then several spools of fencing wire

plus something Arthur was very pleased to see
a new chainsaw of a decent size
he smiled at the thought of Callum
on his somewhat excited spending spree
I reckon you're a bit into this shopping business
don't you reckon
he quipped as they neared the end of the task

the pile of assorted hardware
beside the kitchen looking much larger than it did on the ute
a rumble of amusement came from Sid as Callum replied
*let's just say that it's a lot more fun than getting the groceries
it caused a bit of amusement in at the hardware store too
this last little lot I reckon
you're coming next time though Arthur*

*we gotta get that licence sorted
but by the look of that sky
we might not be going anywhere for a while
me dad was keen for us to get away early this morning
because of what's on the way
now I can see what he means*
Arthur and Sid looked to the west with Callum as he spoke

*smokes
it's on the way all right*
said Sid slowly
his only form of speaking
*they'll be copping it over in the Hill by the look of that
moving slow and steady too
that can be a bit of a worry*

the dark grey front of clouds
enveloped as if a moving wall
the entire western sky
within the distant thing
high and low
patches of ebony
in pools and swirls

no lightning as they gazed at this dark sudden storm
far away from their still warm sunlit morning
no lightning
but a lengthy deep roll of thunder
pealed out across arid plains
stillness and the somehow anxious calm
evaporating in an instant with the arrival of Harry's ute

thought you weren't back out here until next weekend
shouted Callum
above the idling engine with dust rising around them all
true
Harry shouted back through the open window
but the rise is here
haven't ye heard ye goose

so I've swapped me work schedule
checking some lines that need doing over this way
and if it's all right with the new boss here
I thought we'd camp down near that old canoe tree
Harry motioned for Arthur to come closer
partly to introduce him to the others sharing the front seat
Arthur this is Uncle Cecil

and this fella here is me boy Colin
Harry beamed
the slim-limbed boy sat snug
snuggled against the expansive frame of his father
smiling up at Arthur
the thin and grey Uncle Cecil
waved a cigarette-clutching dark elegant hand

smiling broadly and offering
they'll be on the bite those yella-bellies
don't you know
a nice rise comin' through
Uncle Cecil had the whispering rasp of wisdom
a voice of knowledge and cigarettes
his eyes honest and shining

eyes that held also a moist limpid quality
spoke of a life lived
hinted at age and decline
Arthur wanted immediately to talk with him
listen to him
this man of years
yet could think of nothing

had nothing wise or witty to offer
we'd better get down there too then
he concluded finally
Harry put his vehicle back into gear
keen to again be under way
better be quick then by the look of that storm
we're gunna get down there

set up camp
see ye there eh
and he was off
spraying them a little with dust and small stones
a showy spinning U-turn
the cracking throaty laughter of Uncle Cecil
trailing as the ute sped away

once they'd stopped laughing
cursing at the same time
Callum suggested they get down to the river too
even if we just go straight down to the pump Arthur
a rise is something to see
come on
let's head

Callum excitedly led the way back to the ute
Arthur both pleased and disappointed
since he had first arrived
there had been talk of the rise coming down
he sensed the anticipation and excitement in everyone he met
it was mentioned all the time
in the same breath as the weather and a hello

how are ye
hot isn't it eh
there's a rise on the way
shouldn't be long now
another warm one
ye hear the rise is comin
could be a full banker too

all seemed to speak in understated tones
yet by mentioning it always
this thing of water approaching
anticipation clearly conveyed
Arthur excited to know that it was there
flowing into and through
his property

and he knew already what water meant to all out there
yet he felt strangely cheated in some way
having had in his head
the idea that he would be there standing on the bank somewhere
watching the first wave or whatever push on through
he felt excited and a bit anxious as Callum drove his ute
down along the pipe track to the little pump housing

squeezed into the ute's cab
between his friend and the still unknown Sid
wishing he had jumped up on the back tray
hanging on standing up
wind pushing at his face and hair
to be a boy again
riding on the back of his dad's old grey ute

though when they reached the bank
when they pulled up beside the silent green diesel engine
disappointment was far from his mind
each time he had seen the river
little more than a pale brown series of pools
suddenly miraculously before him
a powerful entrancing thing

no thunderous rapids nor spectacular waterfalls
but a swift and strong flow of muddy cream
seemed to pulse from one serpentine bend to the next
steep loamy banks leading down to the sad stagnant pools
disappeared
just a few metres now between the arching racing flow
top of the bank still dusty dry

the three men stood on the soft earth
just a few metres above the wet rampaging thing
Callum could see the delight
wonder on the face of his friend
what do you think of that then Arthur
told you it was a thing to see
Arthur gazed in delight

you're not wrong there
you are not wrong there
insane too
knowing that we've had no rain here
none at all
Callum also gazed at the special thing
every time he witnessed it special still

yeah like I was telling you
this is from the big dump they had up in Queensland
few weeks back
around Charleville and St George
it flows down this way
well
what the cotton farms and whatnot don't grab upstream

comes down through here
with any luck it'll flood out some too
'cause that's what the whole place needs
Callum hurled a small stick into midstream
those back-to-front streams you were talking about
Arthur added
not taking his eyes off the energy pumping by his feet

yeah that's it
that's them
designed to spill out along all these little rivulets
kind of finger out across the plain
so instead of rain falling and then trickles running into streams
and them streams forming up into rivers
it's all a bit back-to-front out here

trouble is though
began a more animated Sid
is that stuff all ever gets to us nowadays
even less to those below
prompting Arthur to ask
because of the cotton
expecting it to be so

yeah they're the big ones
but we're all to blame I reckon too
everyone wants way too much from it
so it's just become this one long drain
supposedly once a big series of wetlands
kind of natural dams that'd hold water
push it out across the land

anyway that's all gone
what does come down now
just goes scooting on by
everyone tries to suck up their bit
quick as they can
then we wonder why there are a few problems
down the years

they had a heap of rain up north you know
this here water now
would've been across all your lovely flood-out country
few years back
and it should be now
we should be hauling this old pump away from here
but I reckon he'll be safe tonight sad to say

Arthur began to see Sid in a different way
his straightforward anger said much
how much he understood and genuinely cared
that country and this river thing
for some time none of them spoke a word
looking at the flow
the frequent pieces of debris

each man separated slightly from the other
following their thoughts
points of interest
along the bank
or amongst the rising and increasing flow
Sid perched himself against the smoothed and aged trunk
a long-fallen red gum

rolling a cigarette in the dry swirling air
now that's no help to a bloke trying to give up the same
called Arthur across to him
having wandered further along the top of the bank
it's a bit of a battle to tell ye the truth
with this wind
I can't see this storm being far away

snake
yelled Callum
from his spot at the water's edge
the others froze momentarily
hoping for more words
gazing at the younger man
pointing and gesturing across the river

there look
straight across there look
swimming straight across
but the current should sweep him a bit beyond us
eh Sid
Sid looked intently
clutching a tobacco pouch and a partly constructed cigarette

scratching his whiskered chin with the other hand
yeah it's got a bit of size about it all right
it should hit the bank a little way away
taipan ye reckon
he asked without looking away
guess so yeah
bit hard to say from here

and I'm fine with not getting close enough to confirm exactly
Sid laughed
no there's no future in chasing them
that's a fact
Arthur gazed in wonder
the way the two men spoke so calmly
about such a dangerous thing

the thing itself a wonder
this dark brown thin line
somehow swishing its way
crossing the mass of water that they dared not enter
the near black streak
against the pale milky coffee-coloured torrent
things of power both

made sense
what Callum said about the current pushing the reptile
far enough away
by the time it reached their side of the bank
yet for a few moments
there was a sense of fragility
in the presence of a thing with the power to swiftly kill

the snake seemed to hover there for a time
straight out from where they were
a safe distance
but there was no comforting exhibition glass between it and them
Arthur followed its progress
until with some relief for all
it found a twisted cluster of tree limbs

within a ramshackle snag
about thirty metres downstream
it disappeared
here it comes now look
Sid called to the others
palms turned skyward
his gaze turning to the dark mass forming above

just a few drops but you can smell it eh
then within a minute of Sid speaking
rain came down
the slow build-up throughout the morning
finally became a few spare drops
before suddenly thundering down
and he could smell it too thought Arthur

it was not the damp thick summer rain smell he knew from the east
rain that breaks humidity
this was a sudden and rich earthy perfume
smell of water and that dusty ochre earth colliding
new to him
that smell as rain
yet it had a familiarity too that he struggled to place

such an evocative thing
yet his memory struggled
a few too many glasses and bottles
lifted to his lips over his not so many years
attempting to remember something
felt at times
as if he were just looking into some kind of void

so much of his past life
spread out like those vast plains around him
endless and parched was his memory
then from the haze somehow
came the flash of a morning not long gone
saw himself again walking up along the dry creek bed
the morning after smash releasing the water in that reservoir

discovery of carvings
heat and a wave of almost nausea
realising the import of his find
all these images
though never since far from his mind
now pushed back into his brain
to the exclusion of all else

Arthur stood there
at the top of a bank long dry
with a river again finally flowing
mightily at his feet
thick bombs of moisture landing with increasing frequency
upon the dusty soil
sparse dry vegetation all around

the smell of rain now upon them
not of the decay of roos
of goats and ancient things
just before on that morning alone
before climbing up through the heat
to the top of the emptied reservoir
he walked by the saturated section of the dry creek bed

that smell not unlike the onset of this much anticipated desert rain
close to the broken wall
everything putrid yes
yet even a little away
where the water had for a time
gushed and attempted to push out
fan out across a sandy creek bed powder-dry

just a few metres away
as if the death
the badness
putrefaction had already been leached away
badness was maybe blown by a morning breeze
dried by the early warm sun
certainly leached through by welcoming dry earth

leaving only the good moist odour
water upon soil
we'll be stuck here real quick
on these soft tracks
suggested Callum as he climbed back behind the wheel
Arthur jumped up onto the back tray of his ute
as the others urged him inside the cab with themselves

you'll be soaked in a flash
it'll come in a hurry now Callum suggested
well you'd better take off then
I'll be right up here Arthur called in reply
as he stood upon the already greasy metal tray
gripping the top bar behind the cab
shirt stuck to skin wet even before they moved away

I thought you fellas out here
Arthur shouted
bending down to the driver's window
supposed to dance around in the rain and stuff
when it finally came
sooks
bloody sooks

a murmur of laughter from the cab below
as Callum drove with haste
back up towards the cluster of dwellings
Arthur standing through the rain increasing
drops hitting like little pleasant needles on his face
saturated as he drank in the pleasure of it all
inhaling deep the thick perfume of rain and a grateful earth

12

no sooner had they arrived at the shearing quarters
scurried across onto the closest veranda
than Harry's vehicle also returned
Harry and young Colin quickly emerged
darted through the sheeting rain to join the other three men
Cecil remained
quiet in the ute

ye leaving the old fella high and dry Harry
asked Callum as they all stood watching
excitedly observing the torrent upon them
his voice becoming a little higher in pitch as he shouted
shouting to be heard above the noise of rain on the bare iron roof
yeah and you try shifting him too
came Harry's loud reply with a smile

he wants to stay put in there
he'll be right
he'll have made sure that his smokes are still dry
still dirty with me he is for coming back now
but that river was fairly pumping through at that bend
down by the canoe tree
might yet come over I reckon

and this rain well
that was it for me
wouldn't fancy being stuck down there with only greasy tracks all around
and the river coming over that bank maybe
the four men and young Colin settled on the veranda
sitting on the steps up into the separate shearers' rooms
or slouched over the mismatched timber chairs

barely speaking
nor attempting to
amid the sound of a storm against a roof of corrugated iron
simply entranced by the deluge they found themselves within
teas and coffees soon turned into cans of beer
as they realised that the storm had set properly in
plans had changed

late in the afternoon
rain slowed enough for a short period
enough to enable Uncle Cecil to emerge from the wet white vehicle
Arthur watched him walk without rush
through the still steady rain
he could no doubt have escaped more moisture
if he chose to move with more speed

Arthur wondered if it was age that slowed him
perhaps an indifference to the elements
or perhaps the rain for Uncle Cecil
a thing to be enjoyed
whatever the reality
he stepped onto the dry veranda floorboards
flicking moisture from a well-loved broad-brimmed leather hat

offering an open smile
Arthur expected some sense of annoyance
from this fellow who had planned to be camped elsewhere
instead came the words of a positive light heart
motioning his hat in Arthur's direction
speaking loudly to all the others
in their various veranda locations

brings a bit a luck with him eh
this fella
real good luck
river down there risen up
now all this lovely rain
good thing you come here boy
or we be still walking round on the dry sand

they all laughed as he moved closer to Arthur
and continued
just you wait now
just you watch this rain turn the whole world green
it's a wonderful thing
my old mum used to say
the earth needs the dry

the earth needs the dry
needs to rest
so she said
and yet it needs all this rain too
this lovely rain
and the river fillin' up too innit
lovely it is eh

Uncle Cecil sighed a restful contented sigh
as he brought a light wooden chair from against the wall
to the edge of the damp veranda
grateful for the shelter
but keen to be as close as could be to the cooling damp fall
well if the dry's all about the earth resting
I reckon she's wide awake now Uncy chortled Harry deep and long

though not always thundering down
rain continued heavily throughout the night
for the first time since Arthur's arrival
his evening meal
could not be prepared across an open fire
instead they took beers into the expansive kitchen
boiling potatoes and frying up steaks just partially thawed

young Colin sat quietly at one end of the large rectangular table
his slight arms supporting the open half-smiling face
listening to the disjointed conversation of men
unnaturally loud due to rain
words echoing in ricochet across the surfaces of kitchen linoleum
though his eyes at times encompassed all
were never very far from his father

you've got a good boy there Harry
Arthur began as the meal concluded
a slight dip in the volume of rain
he spoke loudly so that the boy might also hear
yeah he's all right eh
must be his mother though
quiet and calm I mean

at this young Colin became even more shy
feeling the eyes of all upon him
smiling more broadly
snuggling in to his father's expanse in an embarrassed embrace
that be so
that surely be so Uncle Cecil agreed
a high light giggle breaking his words

a very good woman so is she
his mother there
as if to rescue his son from the unwanted attention
Harry suggested that they have a scrub and get to bed
the boy quickly to his feet
offering soft voiced goodnights
goodnights to all

Harry hastily stacked up the plates and cutlery still on the table
plonked them in the empty sink
saying his loud goodnights
the big man made a suggestion for the day to come
what's say we take Uncy up to that old reservoir in the morning eh
if the rain backs off a bit
me boy here needs to see all that there too I'm keen

Arthur looked across to Callum
whose eyes did not meet his own
then to the face of Uncle Cecil
calm and contemplative
Harry left without discussion
but with nods of approval
trailing behind him from all

Uncle Cecil lit another cigarette
then gone with a silent wave
the drumming of rain
lessened for a time
once again sharpening the volume of conversation
Callum retrieved two more beers from the cool room
Arthur accepted willingly

so much for giving these things away
the two men tapped cold cans together in cheers
as they had so often done before
Arthur's open promise to himself
give up the grog
had not yet gained real traction
maybe tomorrow he suggested once more

he also rolled a cigarette
slouched back comfortably
in the less than comfortable stiff moulded plastic chair
do you reckon we'll get up the creek there
with all this water around
Callum pondered a moment more
somewhat hopeful as he replied

it'll be all right on the bikes I reckon
as long as it's not still bucketing down
slippery yes but not impossible
it'll be a bit of a spin-out though hey
being up there
with Uncle Cecil and young Colin
don't ye reckon

that's a fact agreed Arthur
and it'll be pretty full-on for Harry too
taking them both there
it was tough enough for him when he first saw it all
just with us
and I've been wondering
how it'll all fare in this weather too

them carvings looked so fragile
once that yuk water had been drained away
now all this rain again
maybe choking it back up
damming it all again
if only temporarily
with all sorts of junk no doubt swirling everything all around

same said Callum
I'm not sure I want to think about it
what may or may not be there
exposed now as it all is
open to the elements
and exposed too of course
to all sorts of behaviour of man

Sid had been the first to choose sleep that night
and the next morning first to rise
when Arthur emerged
only just dawn
yet a pot of tea ready to share
and the smell of toast under way
filled the kitchen

nothing's as good I reckon
as the sleep I get with rain on the roof
sleep all right yourself Arthur then
Arthur rubbing eyes as he slumped down at the table
still waking
the smooth tabletop felt cool and a little moist
he noticed that the rest of the kitchen had also been cleaned

dishes done
things put away and benches wiped
Sid appeared almost jovial amid his domesticity
yeah all right
replied Arthur a little guarded
*Callum and I had a few too many beers
but there's nothing new there*

well you might want to ration them a bit old son
suggested Sid
*we won't be going anywhere for a while
given the rain we've had
and that includes getting in to the pub*
he poured a stiff-looking brew of tea for them both
no better time for resting up proper than when you get a good dump of rain

Arthur had not contemplated being isolated for any period of time
but could see how it might now so easily be
it hasn't let up much has it
and as he spoke
as if on cue
the soft drizzle that had been falling since he awoke
turned swiftly once more into heavy rain

both men glanced out through the window
above the double kitchen sink
water sheeted down
morning for a time became darker again
soon Harry appeared
quiet
waking as he walked

they discussed the rain
the likelihood of their isolation for a couple of days
even if the wet were to stop right then
regardless all were still keen to get up to the reservoir that morning
once the rain lifted a little
it was decided that Sid would drive Uncle Cecil in Arthur's ute
the others would travel on bikes

young Colin should be okay on the back with his dad
though he had not done this before
Uncle Cecil emerged from the single room he had chosen
at the veranda's end
he grabbed a chair from the array of mismatched timber and plastic shapes
moved it back against the wall
there he sat and lit his first cigarette of the day

from inside the kitchen Harry sensed a whiff of the tobacco
keen to check on his uncle
see how he felt about the day ahead
he watched the aged man for a moment from the kitchen doorway
ageing lean limbs crossing over each other
in a familiar comfortable way
his whole slight form surrounded by a blue-grey tobacco haze

as Harry moved down closer to him
Cecil spoke without shifting his gaze from the saturated fireplace
beyond the shelter of the veranda
lovely rain innit Harry
Harry stood leaning against a post
near the figure of the quiet older man
that it is Uncy that it is

still feel up for checking out these carvings and that there
it's wet for sure
but we should get up that way all right I'm thinkin'
if ye keen
Uncle Cecil was quiet for a moment before breathing out a steady long sigh
oh I'll be seein' 'em all right
an I'll be lookin' for seein' 'em right today rain or no

Harry looked down at the man he had always respected
so admired
he seemed even older and frailer somehow
suddenly
his uncle gazed out still onto the damp simple muddy courtyard
gazed at the central pool
that had yesterday been a pit for hot coals glowing

in fact Harry
I been seein' 'em seein' 'em all night somehow in me dreams
Callum emerged onto the veranda
next to where Harry stood
he had half heard their words
and so moved towards them
sensed that he had perhaps broken in on something

an awkward pause
then an attempt to slink away down the veranda
but Uncle Cecil would have none of that
mornin' sleepy one
big day comin' up
yed better get a feed in
now you had ye beauty sleep

says you surviving on cigarettes for how many years
Harry laughed at Uncle Cecil
shaking his smooth bald head amused
Callum moved in along to the kitchen without speaking
thinking of just how big a day it might really be
and so they were all soon away
toast and tea and coffee amid a thread of anxiety

a breakfast slightly hurried so that they could all get away
for a moment the rain even stopped entirely
Sid brought up the ute
close to the end of the veranda for Uncle Cecil to hop in
Harry Callum and Arthur jumped on their bikes
young Colin clinging tight in behind his dad's torso
Callum led the way along the top of the slight ridge

Harry next and then Arthur behind
Sid followed the track as best he could
a little lower down
leaving it here and there to seek some rockier stretches
less likely to slide
using an animal track when he could
to anchor the bottom side

Arthur couldn't believe how much the ground had changed
dust and fine pink sand he had before traversed
now a darker sludge
his motorbike slipped often as he became used to it
noticed that both Callum and Harry in front of him
more than a few times also
had a steadying foot placed upon the ground

they proceeded though
before long were up at the shambles that was once a reservoir
they stopped near the base of the broken wall
though the bikes could have gone further up
any ute would have to pull up there
so it was there that they waited for Sid and Uncle Cecil
they hoped not far behind

a steady flow of silt-brown water
swirling from the crude opening
begun by Arthur's handiwork just a few days before
you did a job on it all right Arthur
that you did said Callum as they stood on the upper part of the bank
watching the water pulse from the hole
broaden out to a purling flow several metres wide

Arthur felt a sense of relief that it was at least flowing
so worried the night before
even as they rode the slippery muddy way up there
worried carvings would be immersed again
somehow he had pictured carcasses
other debris re-plugging the gap
causing the whole gully to back up once more

only worse this time
bits of timber and bones
tapping against the fragile artworks
tumbling in the muddy flooding currents
yet it was not so
despite the crudeness of what he had done
a huge relief to see such flow

at least it hasn't backed up again
hey Harry
I was worried about that given the dump we've had
suggested Callum
as if speaking the thoughts of Arthur
yeah well it's coming out steady all right but let's wait and see
could be a bit in there I reckon

Harry looked down along the creek
peering through the steady rain
peering through the light bush that clung to the fringe of the small creek
anxious for the ute to make those final few metres
deliver a treasured uncle to him
so they could be under way
so the old man could see what he had seen

Sid had done well
the vehicle arrived
both Sid and Uncle Cecil laughing at the bumps
at the one final slight slide to a stop
I reckon we won't go up the top eh
Harry suggested in contrast seriously
a bit steep for Uncy up that way I'm thinkin'

just go straight up stream
through the back of it
way we walked out last time eh instructed Harry
without speaking all concurred
Harry and Colin leading the way
a careful but steady Uncle Cecil close behind
following his nephew

there was no track as such through the sparse bush
traced though it was with lines meandering
the work of hooves
sheep and goats
tracks mostly parallel to the now steady flow of the creek
so often dry
now grappling with moisture

Callum Sid and Arthur followed in a line along these grooves
dodging them when deeper puddles formed
here's a good example for you Arthur
the impact these animals have had here
Callum spoke quietly as they walked
slowly behind Uncle Cecil
it's only the introduced species that cause all this

hard hooves of sheep
cattle and goats
not to mention pigs
god you'll know it when you see somewhere they've been
really rip the place up
roos and none of the natives leave scarring like this
all soft-footed you see

yet long after the sheep and cattle are gone these tracks will be here
see how it's changing all this water flow
how it's messed up this whole little creek system here
and the goats are still here of course
they need to go mate and soon too
they don't belong here
not for this soft soil out here

and how was your steak last night Callum
enjoy your beef last night did you
was it lamb the night before taunted Sid
ye come back to us a greenie have ye eh
we can all live off wombats and wallaby stew
save the planet eh and he laughed his rough laugh
expecting a reaction from the young man

it's the balance of what we do Sid
that's all
you know what I mean
you've seen enough of it I reckon
just look at this little example for chrissake
Callum was not angry but clearly unamused
they walked on in silence

Arthur watched both men in front of him
their differing views of the land
almost visible thought bubbles above their silent brooding heads
Arthur watched Uncle Cecil and then up further Harry and his boy
he wondered what they were thinking and feeling
as they walked along the muddy tracks of sheep and goats to view the damage
done by that other species so recently introduced onto that fragile land

there were no tears from Uncle Cecil as he stood at the base of the overhangs
looking at such special things for the first time
no tears but a sad silence
Harry stood beside him
holding young Colin by his hand
Harry simply pointed broadly
both sides of the small rocky ravine

stone held ancient carved images
Uncle Cecil moved away
moved in closer to the first ones he saw
without touching a thing
moved his long slender hands
over shapes as he found them
putting his face up close in the shadows of the gully to better see

after looking intently at the first example he found
a cluster of arcing lines parallel
glanced back to Harry and young Colin
saw them watching him
turned back again to further discover this awful gorgeous treasure
Harry content for a moment just to stand there
with his son

but young Colin soon began pulling at his hand
urging him to follow in behind Uncle Cecil
stinking debris piled along the base before the rain
still there but now supported slightly by water again
the tangled mass bobbed slowly as Harry tried his weight
stepped on a larger piece of timber
so as to hop across to the other side

tentatively did he succeed
urging Colin along behind
so that they could work their way along
along the narrow rocky space
parallel to Uncle Cecil
then would they be only a few metres apart
on each side of the wet gallery

Callum Arthur and Sid seemed content to wait a moment
before Harry had moved too far along Callum called across to him
looks like water has backed up a bit in there again with this rain Harry
do you reckon she's dammed up a bit and then gone back down again
Harry looked around and up above him
hard to say
it's all wet all over

but you'd think at first it would've
when the first heavy rain hit all at once
might have to get your mate there to make a bigger hole eh
Harry smiled and went on
one thing notice Callum said Arthur more quietly
it doesn't smell half as bad
now it's been flushed out a bit

Callum nodded approvingly
that's a fact
a good thing too
it was pretty rich up here Sid
you should've smelt it the other day
much better now
that's a fact

Sid followed along behind Uncle Cecil
Callum and Arthur chose to hop across to the other side
near Harry and young Colin
all took their own time to look at the display of shapes before them
the only words spoken were some quiet comments
explanations from Harry to his son
all soon standing in the gloomy light at the base of the two large boulders

the natural bulk of what had become a dam wall
Uncle Cecil pulled at the heavy metal chain
anchored from the top and still held fast
some kind of valve or shoot hidden below
hidden within the remaining pool of debris and slime
he gazed up along the mess
moving its bulk just slightly

Arthur noticed the scuff marks of his feet
towards the top in the slime
felt an embarrassed flush at the thought of him trying to dive down
just a few days before
the smell of it
the moment of panic below the water revisited him
stayed for an awkward moment

no one else knew of his clumsy attempts at action
no one else had noticed the marks
Uncle Cecil pointed out to all
damage the chain had caused
midway along the metal length
at the outer most point in the boulder's bulging arc
faint remains of a carving

perhaps an eagle
and the others concurred
ten or so deep scraping horizontal arcs just a few inches long
etched by the slow heavy submerged fumbling of chain
metal against carving since 1954
Arthur watched Uncle Cecil look up along the chain
attempting to make out exactly what it was that had been lost

an eagle he repeated *bilyara*
looks like bilyara
other stuff too there but no way to know what now
the elderly man scanned the other side where Harry had led his son
looked at the many works that he had not yet seen up close
took a step back so that his eyes could look properly
the two large boulders with their smears of cement

rough cement used to plug all observed gaps high and low
cement scars to form the crazy reservoir thing
Uncle Cecil looked once again to the chain
hanging there now a forlorn useless thing
just a few decades before
cast so deliberately
so ignorantly across carvings done by hands thousands of years before

of all the things to sadden someone in that small damp ravine
it was the chain that seemed to hurt Uncle Cecil
vandals he spoke softly
just enough for the group at the base of the reservoir wall to hear
vandals them fellas eh
he looked to Harry
who put his large arm around the quivering slight shoulders of the ageing man

13

it was a fair effort
to dam that all up
fair bit of concrete in it altogether when you look at it
a decent effort
do all that
back in the fifties
don't ye reckon

all had been silent since their return
through the ceaseless rain to the cluster of buildings
all but Uncle Cecil were again in the kitchen
gathering biscuits and cups of tea
Uncle Cecil sat outside at the same chair as before
smoking and coughing
looking out into the rain

Arthur wondered if Sid was being his regular blunt self
or speaking with deliberate provocation
he noticed Callum and Harry exchange wry smiles
before Harry took a moment and then replied
yeah a big effort
true
no denying that

a few fellas would've worked hard for a few days on that I reckon
plus don't forget all that metal pipe to lay
right down here to the house too
there must be three or four ks in it eh
but like
a pretty fair effort to carve all that up in there too
all that up there carved in stone using stone tools

and a long time before the bloody fifties
eh Sid
when them things were done up there
to which Sid defended
and I'm not sayin' it ain't
it's amazing
all that up there

it's amazing what they did
just struck me also what a heap a work it would've been
actually dam that thing
that's all
I know it's not what we went up to look at but I dunno
I can't help that
what it made me think about

vandals was the word right enough
Uncle Cecil was spot on I reckon
suggested Callum
Sid stirred some more
it was a different time Callum
them fellas didn't realise what they were doing
they were trying to survive out here

workin' hard to try to make a go of it out here
that's all
it's a bit rich don't ye reckon
lumping today's way of thinking on them back then
it was a different world mate
another pause from all
as if breaths could be heard competing

that be true Sid
that be true Harry began again
shifting up in his seat
large hands flat against the table
palms pressing down
but it's what they did not value that hurts I guess
so it does

and the damage done
forever done up there
I mean
how is that there ever gonna be repaired
might all crack up and fall away once it's dry
and it'll be dry
hot again soon enough as ye know

bad as it is now
might soon totally fall away
Sid turned to Arthur
and what are ye gunna do about water
now you've stuffed your main reservoir
making a point to all
Arthur noticing Uncle Cecil at the door

none of them knew how long he had been there
listening
your wife
Sid
a Paarkintji woman
from my wife's mob too eh
down Menindee way innit

there was a silent pause that none wished to fill
Uncle Cecil settled his slight frame down at the table
beside Arthur
Sid sat across from them
nodding quietly and then raising his face to meet that of the older man
no anger
but an undertow of emotion in the voice of Uncle Cecil as he proceeded

so I'm thinkin'
I'm wonderin'
how it must make you feel
see that up there
all those images and stories
hidden away like that
taken away like that from our people

from your wife's people
for so long
Uncle Cecil waited a moment for a response which came
jesus Unc it's crook all right
real bad what's happened to all that stuff
and Kathy and her sisters if they were here
they'd be howlin' about it too and rightly so

Sid was clearly angered
yet did not like the thought of upsetting Uncle Cecil
but you also admire the handiwork of them fellas back then
them whitefellas I mean challenged Harry some more
Sid stood up as if to help himself breathe a little better
shook his head in exasperation
rinsed his mug at the kitchen sink

the room seemed increasingly small
rain still steady outside
the conversation seeming to circle in on him
he decided to say something more before walking out the door
when I look at the work some of the old-timers out here put in
I do admire it yes
can't help meself

there's nothing wrong surely in that
honouring or at least acknowledging
those who gone before ye eh
but do I wish they'd not damaged all those carvings
well of course I bloody do
but water's the thing
water's the thing

and ye can bet that there's nowhere else on this place
nowhere else to build anything like that reservoir
so my question remains
what's Arthur gunna do about his bloody water storage now
and Sid walked out the door
Harry's words following him
funny time to be worryin' about water when we're drownin' in the stuff

Arthur surprised himself by speaking his mind
without thinking he found himself looking at Uncle Cecil and asking
I was worried how you'd react to all that up there
Uncle Cecil
felt sick when I saw it all at first
other day
so I was wondering how it was going to hit you

the older man had been looking at Arthur intently
continued thus as he thought about a response
eyes scanned the room
looked up and around the sparse yet tidy room
resting on nothing
looking up and around
as if mustering his ideas

oh it hit me
it did hit me too
still is
still is sinking in I reckon eh
but I dunno about angry
sad more than angry I reckon
I'm beyond anger maybe

I've seen enough bad stuff to be beyond anger
sad though for what has been lost
sad that so many of our people
so many not seen this before they gone
his eyes now rested back on Arthur
a different kind of man somehow
a fella you could talk plainly to

I mean I didn't even know of that little gully up there
such an important place like that
and I didn't know it there
none of our old people do
and here Harry broke in somewhat animatedly
that's the thing
the thing that hurts so much

I don't know that old Sid will ever see
ever get it
so much of our knowledge
so comprehensively taken away
all that learning is gone see
they are not simply things to be preserved
though that has to be our job from now on

they are markers of land
the template for stories
oh we can study it now
even get experts in from somewhere
interpret it all they want
but the oral stuff's gone
too much of that circle broken

there followed several moments of awkward quiet
Callum collected the tea mugs from all
rinsed them at the sink
looked through the simple window at the rain still coming down
unusually quiet thought Arthur
but he suspected perhaps Callum knew
someone who sensed when it was wise to be quiet

as if to break a sadness that was descending
Uncle Cecil rose to leave
withdrawing cigarettes from his shirt breast pocket as he did
on his way to the door he stopped behind Arthur
placing a hand on his shoulder and asked
and so what will you do lucky fella
what will ye do with this place

this special place
with all ye money eh
do ye think money can fix what's been done here eh
and the elderly man walked quietly away
leaving Arthur feeling emptier still
the word money actually made Arthur physically weak
at least the way Uncle Cecil said it

he had bent down close to his ear
squeezed the word out slowly
making him recoil a little
Arthur was beside Callum on one side of the large white kitchen table
opposite Harry and his boy
Colin sat with his little legs crossed beneath him on the chair
exploring his father's mobile phone for photos and games

Harry then spoke to his friends new and old
lots to do you could say
lots to do
with a swift response from Arthur
emphasising Uncle Cecil's troublesome word
lots to do with my money you mean
lots to do with my awful money

don't take offence at Uncy there Arthur
Harry followed
lots of people don't like the stuff
have seen so much of it wasted out here too
he's just having a little dig at ye that's all
to which Arthur bluntly replied
and fair enough too I reckon

something good had better come from all this money of mine
prompting a thoughtful pause from all
before Callum put in
what do you think about the water Harry
heaps of new tanks
or even just a couple of big ones up on the ridge would do it
don't ye reckon

yeah but I dunno
out here that all takes a fair bit of money eh
quipped Harry cheekily
to a little laughter from all as he continued
yeah no Sid's right to be worried about storing water Arthur
but ye can fix it with a bunch of well placed new tanks
like Callum's saying

I mean there's nothin' wrong with the pump
set-up from the river as it is
but when you add it all up
there's a mile of roofs that should be catching good rainwater for the house
I'd be looking at setting that right too bud
ye can't pump from the river now when it's in flood
neither can ye when it's way down low

which is most of the time let me tell ye
so yeah a few tanks wouldn't go astray eh
Arthur sat up a little on his hard plastic seat
elbows on the cool table top
talk of specifics made his spirits lift somewhat
he didn't know exactly where to commence
such a huge list of tasks ahead of him

he didn't really even yet know the list
at least not the full extent
let alone how to give things some form of logical priority
so this talk of water
solving a problem from someone he trusted
was nothing less than a tonic
he wanted to be a part of the plan

the homestead didn't seem to have any major water damage
when I had a pretty good look around the other day
maybe we should check it out properly
don't even remember noticing the gutters to tell you the truth
at which Harry grinned
well now would be the time to have a good look at water flowing
if it eases off enough for us to scoot over there that is

I mean before this rain here
we hadn't had a decent drop in over a year
and not a proper soak and a rise in the river since I can't remember when
so now when all the gutters or what's left of them are full
now's the time to be checking
peering out the window above the sink Callum suggested
it might be easing off a little

let's take a couple of beers and go for a wander eh
I reckon it'd be a top spot over on that big wide veranda in the rain
you might even see the river from there
sweeping around that big wide bend full to the bank
all agreed to make the move
Arthur's pleasure at the thought of progress obvious to all
at least a few steps along the long path ahead of him

Harry plonked a football cap on Colin's head
they stepped out into the steady though softer rain
pulled his own on a little more firmly
walking beside Arthur he sensed the spark in his step
ye like it out here don't ye bud
he commented without expecting a reply
Arthur thought for a minute in silence

looking at Callum up ahead breaking into a jog
a six-pack of cans dangling from each hand
yeah I do
there seems to be a whole lot to like
and as you said earlier
a whole lot to do
Harry grinned and laughed some more as he replied

just to me seems like a hell of a place to choose
having so much money and all
I mean
a bloke who wins the lottery
in Newcastle wasn't it
a fella could've bought a flash place on the beach right there
or down on Sydney Harbour eh

with a boat parked out the front
but not you eh
you picked Leopardwood on the Paaka
funny fella this one here Colin
good bloke but a bit funny
Colin glanced between both smiling men
his small hand deep in the warmth of his father's

kirinya did you say
the word for the leopardwood tree
Arthur called as he broke into a run
dashing the last twenty yards or so onto the shelter of the wide veranda
maybe I've been floating around long enough
just glad to wash up some place where there's lots to do
endless good work

14

the veranda was a welcome calm
three men and a boy gravitated to the north-west corner
the point most likely to catch a glimpse of the torrent below
and they were not disappointed
the house was set lower down the slight barren ridge
lower than the cluster of shearers' quarters buildings
closer to the river

enough elevation from which to watch the light brown flow
see it arc somehow round another wide serpentine bend on its journey south
top spot Arthur
Callum offered with enthusiasm
I can picture you up here
once you fix it all up
looking down upon your kingdom

you normally wouldn't see the water as well as this of course
but you'd see a bit unless it was really low
no this is awesome hey Harry he concluded
as Callum distributed beers they took up positions of relative comfort
sitting on the timber floorboards
Colin had managed to climb up onto a large sandstone lookout
blocks that formed supports for the central entranceway

he looked happy to be up much higher than the men
standing up on the stonework for a time
from there an even better view of what lay below
leaving the men to their silly drinks
notice anything about this here veranda too quizzed Harry
Callum and Arthur shook their heads quietly
expecting some kind of joke from the large happy man

it's dry he said flatly
holding a hand out upwards as if checking for rain
good roof I'm thinkin' Arthur
good rainwater-catching-for-storage roof you have here
Callum adding
whole place looks pretty sound to me
gutters maybe shot but you might be better to leave the roof just as is

we'll hop up and check it out once it dries off a bit
Harry looked beyond the river
I don't know that it's gunna pull up in a hurry
more black in the sky over there look
I'm thinking we won't be going anywhere for a few days eh
to which Callum suggested
plenty of time to sit and think about this place maybe

well that's it innit smiled Harry
a bit of enforced planning time Arthur
and how many beers ye got here anyway
they all laughed and offered up a perfunctory cheers
all happy for a short time to gaze out through the steady rain
collecting their thoughts
glimpses of the river brimming at the top of its high damp banks

unusually it was Arthur who rekindled the conversation
though he didn't know how to say it
he could think of nothing better than to be right there
on that veranda beginning to feel his own
with the other two men and young Colin
the rain and all that was happening with the river
simply made him feel even more alive

ye reckon Uncle Cecil will be all right
his question directed to Harry
I mean it's pretty full-on isn't it
those carvings and all for him
Harry thought and took another sip from his can of beer
oh it's full-on all right that it is
Uncy'll be fine but yeah ye gotta feel for him a bit

I mean it hurts us all what happened up there
what them fellas did decades ago eh
whitefellas too
I reckon it's hard for you fellas seein' that stuff too eh
but for Uncle Cecil's generation well I dunno
they have lost so much ye know
Christ they were even taken themselves them stolen ones

it seems so unreal lookin' back on it from here
but there ye go
she all happened
it really happened all that an' so all that there
all those carvings swallowed up by that stinky water for so long
all them paintings too that I reckon would've been in there for sure
now totally gone

all that has gotta be real hard for the likes of Uncle Cecil
a bit like well what else ye gonna throw at me eh
so in ye face
all that bad stuff
an' he were right I reckon
callin' it vandalism that's what it is
cultural vandalism

Callum responding steadily and thoughtfully
I tell ye what I don't get Harry
I don't get how he can be as calm and forgiving as he is
you too for that matter
Harry answered easily
looking at his son
jumping on and off the high stonework a few metres away

well the alternative ain't real flash
gettin' aggro
all arced-up is something Uncle Cecil and me have done before
but it doesn't seem to get anyone very far
and besides that Callum
said Harry with a broad smile
we're so used to you whitefellas disappointing us disgusting us

following some laughter from all
Harry continued seriously
no I reckon Uncy up there
I reckon Uncy will be right now up there
suckin' in a smoke an' workin' on a way through this
he'll be thinkin' about the best way
best way we can be together on this place

might also have a whole list of people in his head
people he wants to come and see so look out Arthur
to which the improbable owner replied
he can invite the whole mob if he wants
plenty of room
what eight rooms over at the shearers' quarters
and a bit of space for camping you could say

Harry seized the chance for a dig
oh I was thinkin' a doin' this place up a bit for ye
smiling sideways across to Callum
I reckon I could fit a heap a me cousins in this here old girl
this old house here
that'd spark the place up a bit
Arthur smiled at the thought

all in good time Harry all in good time
I do want to do this place up
it's a fair size but I dunno
feels good somehow this house
just look at how your Colin's into it there
Colin had found that he could stand on the stonework
just able to reach a roof beam to swing from

Harry called out for him to take care
yeah he'll find something to amuse himself anywhere
a physical kid ye know
doesn't have his face in these little computer games all the time
so many buried in screens nowadays eh even his age
prompting Callum to query
how old is he now Harry

they all watched Colin scamper up and down the small stone supports
five turned five a few weeks back
replied the proud parent
I was watching him the other day
over at a little park in the Hill
they had one of them fake rock climbing wall things
ye know with them bits of moulded plastic knobs to climb up

well this little fella stands at the bottom
must have been three times the height of himself too
sizes it up a bit and off he goes
picking his way straight up to the top
couldn't believe it
no way known I'd get up it meself
but there he went up and over

amazing how they grow up really
Colin sensed all eyes were upon him
stopped playing and returned to the side of his father
sitting on the veranda floorboards dusty pink
back against the wall with legs outstretched
can I have a drink he asked
reaching at Harry's can of beer

no fear little man ye not startin' on this stuff
not if I can help it
there's your little bottle there look
and the boy drank thirstily
from the plastic bottle of water his father had brought for him
I saw a fella the other day give their kid a swig of grog
no more than Colin here I reckon

it might've been in that same park come to think of it yeah
lettin' his little fella have a drink of beer
just so he could look like a big man in front of his mates I reckon
how could ye do that eh
Harry's friends simply nodded as they drank more themselves
you'll have to get yourselves some kids you two
they're the best thing little ones

there followed a slight awkward pause as Callum glanced at Harry
as if to warn him off the topic
Harry gave a short nod
he hadn't forgotten the little that he knew about Arthur's past
though he felt that Callum was being over-sensitive as always
he got it and so shut up
quietly drinking some more

I nearly did get there once
Arthur replied just as Callum was struggling to think of something to throw in
to change the topic entirely
how's that then asked Harry
not wanting to betray what Callum had divulged to him
I was married
my wife was hit by a car

she was expecting our bub
what is it four close to five years ago now
Arthur sat looking out at the sweep of country beyond the veranda
punctuating the scene
the wet expanse
flashes of his Beth
each time he blinked

each time he blinked in his slow relaxed way
came forth a flash memory of his dead wife
smiling close up to his own face
on the afternoon she told him about the child to be
a smile of fear and joy
her lovely soft round face
his Beth he had not cherished enough before all the tears

full-on bud said Harry deeply
he had the ability Arthur had observed
usually reserved
for the possessor of a very large resonating chest
the ability to speak deeply yet softly when it was required
you've been through something there all right
that is something

they all now looked out across the swollen river arc
feeling more at ease not locking eyes
instead listening intently respectfully
aah seems like a while ago now
other times not
a fragile thing though isn't it
life

all life when you think about it
and I guess like lots of people
it wasn't until I lost Beth that I got it
you get it Harry just look at this beaut little man here
Colin squirmed a little again
his father and these two other men
all looking at him with their concerned kind eyes

he turned in towards Harry some more snuggling in
prompting light laughter from the men
a welcome release valve to the tension
the anxiety that had come with their words
I just don't understand how it isn't treasured
it's such a fragile thing
how can life not be cherished said Arthur with visible exasperation

and life in all forms too when you think on it entered Callum
it's all spectacularly improbable when you think about it
and all interconnected too
Harry laughed *steady up*
Sid'd be callin' ye a greenie by now
and guilty as charged mate guilty as charged Callum went on
it is all interconnected the whole world of course it is

water
soil erosion the carbon cycle
we are all stardust and all that
plus he said with even more emphasis
plus we should be treasuring the stuff that matters
the stuff that is left behind
Arthur was content to listen and to ponder

but Harry could not help himself
what like snakeskins and cicada shells
and maybe the broken bits of concrete in that old reservoir eh
maybe that rusty old pipe over there eh
Callum as always was up for the spar
snakeskins and cicada shells
yes a certain beauty to them

but when you talk about the legacy of man
I was thinking more about those carvings than the dam wall
they're treasures without me even understanding them properly
not just because they are so old but also I reckon
because they're expressions of life
and they kind of enhance that space not detract from it
Harry nodded and Arthur formed his thoughts as they left his mouth

some of these buildings I like
these big old shady verandas
the original stone building behind there
even the way some of the sheds and little structures are scattered around
they kind of make sense I reckon
agreed said Harry promptly
as much as I hate to agree with Sid on anything

and I'm sure he'd be singin' your praises right there bud
as long as you don't let him know I said so
I like this sort of stuff too
stone and timber by clever human hands innit
simple and belongs here seems now
different things mind
this here nice shady veranda and them carvings thousands of years old

and listen
if we're not careful
this rain looks like stopping for good eh
Harry announced to all
helping his son as he clambered across high veranda stonework once more
might go and check out a few of these structures
these Colonial National Treasures belonging to Arthur here

whata ye say
the rain did cease and they did explore
yet of all the sheds and small outbuildings they made their way to
only one
a relatively new-looking chicken enclosure
was wet through and in need of repair
all seemed empty but for the dust inside dry

deserted spaces with the exception of an old small square structure
the slaughter house
a single rather menacing-looking hook
still hanging stiffly from a rust-tarnished flat metal rail
then stables and the old blacksmiths right beside
with what seemed like a huge number of tools still there
now this is the business

so announced Harry as they swung back the loosely closed double doors
just room for three men and a boy to stand
between the doorway and the centrepiece of the dusty space
the forge
in here too the rain had been kept at bay
a puddle at the entrance
where ground had been trodden down through the years

check this out Harry enthralled
if you can see through the dust
fair bit here
the dust was more than a coating
it was layered as if sheets of filigree
films across the benches of hand tools large and small
some objects hung from the walls on either side

many others lay scattered across the workbenches
in some sections organised into neat clusters
the small forge also
its coals resting there long cold
bellows gaping expectantly
an unused treasure
not one useless thing

pretty tidy really
considering how long it must be since it was used
like they had a big clean-up before shutting it down the last time
Callum observed
picking up a hammer
tapping it lightly
observing dust fall

Harry and Arthur didn't touch a thing
just took it all in slowly
working out the use of the different shapes
the sense of purpose within the room
young Colin picked up a horseshoe from a small pile
felt its weight in his small hands
attempted to balance it on the anvil he straddled

he asked his father what it was
then if he could keep it
Harry turned to Arthur as if to check that it was okay
Arthur thankful for the poor filtered light
as he stood away from the door feeling himself flush brightly
awkward that he should be the one in charge
responsible for any of these objects so new to him too

nor could he recall the last time he had a possession worthy of giving away
embarrassed also
to have a Paarkintji man ask his permission for anything on that land
of course he finally put out the words in the hope that all would move on
imagine being in here in the summer
with this thing cranked up eh said Harry looking closer at the forge
fancy having this little fella lit up when it's forty degrees outside

Callum and Arthur murmured agreement
continued to paw over objects large and small with their eyes
Colin had soon seen enough and was outside
washing his new metal prize in the wide shallow entranceway pool
in time the men followed
Arthur somewhat proudly relatched the door
sensing that it was a space to which he would often return

perhaps tidy up
perhaps leave as it was
a kind of time capsule
a physical link to those who had worked so hard on the place before
you're a smart fella all right Arthur
comin' here in autumn
said Harry as they moved back towards the main house

best time I reckon right now usually
but summer can be a bit hard
unless you're used to it
and even if you are it can be full on
February we had seventeen days on the trot over forty
that slowed us down a bit I can tell ye
a local like me too

Harry stopped abruptly
sunshine
I think that our little dose of precipitation may have finally moved on
looking up at the homestead he smiled and pointed out to Arthur
just look at your joint Arthur
sittin' up there sparklin' freshly washed in the sun
looks good eh the old place

they walked slowly back towards the large house
Arthur agreed
he knew that it needed a heap of work
to make it a home
but even that was a good thing it seemed to him just then
he nodded and smiled in agreement
yet said nothing

have you had a good look in the little old stone house Arthur
asked Callum *let's have a look in there eh*
see how it fared in all this rain
Callum striding ahead without waiting for the others to agree
he turned and walked backwards for a moment as he continued cheekily
you can go in first if you like Harry
in case that big brown snake's somewhere in under all that lovely sandstone

Callum and Arthur both laughed
Harry decidedly unamused
an' why the hell did you have to mention that snake
you'll scare the boy here
thus causing even more amusement
oh the boy
of course the boy mocked Callum

once closer though
all were on their guard
once between the homestead and the older stone building
eyes scanned before steps were taken
yet there was no sign of a snake
even the tracings in the dust
washed away by the welcome rain

several well-placed stepping stones linked buildings
spanned a gap between the two structures
the group stood together in the crisp shade of the simple veranda
Callum placed his hands against the single timber rail
leaning his weight against it
perhaps once painted or given a stain
many summers had weathered what was in his hands

they're all great buildings when you look at it eh he began
I mean
even though you've got two houses here close together
they kind of work
if ye know what I mean
maybe it's just these verandas everywhere
the simple stone and timber I dunno

to which Harry concurred
plus the aspect
those old fellas thought things through
a lot more than most newer stuff if ye ask me
just look at this little place
nice big veranda with thick stone walls
and a ceiling as high as they could make it

a door at the front and back for whatever breeze to sneak on through
and ye can bet it'll be facing north exactly
perfect I reckon
lovely and cool with a nice big old stove in there for winter look
and what do ye see goin' up now nine times outa ten
prefab garbage that has to be air-conditioned
bollocks to that

I grew up in a house like this
me old aunty and I lived in a house like this in town there
a bit the worse for wear but lovely it was just the same
all walked inside the single room
the air was cooler as if illustrating Harry's words
with a dustiness for having been closed for so long
yet not unpleasantly so

a door at the back as Harry had suggested
to the side of the blackened wood fuel stove
the object that occupied most of the large hearth
the structure's centre stage
well worn with dust encasing
still looked as if it would welcome a fire
its heavy front doors of different sizes shut firm

some objects left behind
though not the treasure trove of tools at the smithy's
some furniture
a single timber table and four bentwood chairs
then atop the cooker a heavy black frying pan
three deep rectangular tins stacked together
awaited a baker's hands

near the hearth the floor was also of stone
smoothed yet not evenly
it gave a crisp scuffing sound to Arthur as he stepped
moved closer to open a heavy small door of the cooker
as with the blacksmith's shop
all had been left intact and tidy
sealed with the dust of years

wonder how many loaves of bread and Sunday roasts this thing has turned out
he asked as the others watched him peering into the fire box
beyond the reach of the stone hearth the floor was timber
but of a very narrow board
Callum offered his thoughts on this
perhaps a local hardwood variety
roughly milled by someone here

a slightly darker border
two feet or so running to the skirting boards
Japan Black suggested Callum
applied beyond the border of a single carpet rug square
a rug long disappeared somewhere
yet Arthur could picture another
placed on the still solid boards sometime soon

not a sign of moisture anywhere Arthur
you could do worse than set up camp in here
at least while you work on the main house suggested Harry
they emerged again into the sunlight and now almost clear blue skies
I was thinking the very same Arthur replied
it's a top little spot I reckon yeah
and I could graft away steady at the house

Harry seemed to pause before he began again
an comin' from me this might sound a bit weird
but it's hard to imagine these buildings not being here
maybe it's because of the local stone
the timber and that there I dunno
but they're sure not a scar on the land at least
and that's somethin' innit

15

Sid surprised all as they encountered him
standing out on the front veranda of the main house
leaning against the blond stone
supports young Colin had not so long before been clambering upon
he had heard their voices
echoing in swirls around the buildings for some moments
not sure exactly where they were

he turned and looked up to face them
as the front door began to open and they emerged
well
just when I thought there was no furniture left in the place
here's some out here look Harry joked
an old piano and now Sid
well there ye go eh

all were amused
including Sid who appreciated Harry's humour
a kind of lifeline to help him get back on board
still holding some anxiety about the way their last conversation had ended
but there without Uncle Cecil for a while
he might have a chance to explain better what he meant
about the legacy of those who had gone before

looks like we've all had the same idea
checking the place out a bit
Sid suggested once the light laughter at his expense had subsided
it's quite a joint you've taken on here Arthur
quite a thing
Arthur smiled with a mixture of shyness and pride
sensing the eyes of Callum and Harry also upon him

yeah thanks
and they knew how to build things didn't they
this old girl's been closed up for a few years
but no real leaks or damage we've found
just a bit in the chook house out the back
have ye seen the old smithy shop Sid Harry asked
not without excitement

no I just went for a bit of a wander
then heard your voices up this way replied Sid
well that's one place ye need to check out
still full of stuff like they just walked out the door
full a dust too of course like everywhere Harry enthused
that's it of course a few dust storms every year
no one here to look after the place

Sid stood with legs apart
hands pushed down into work jeans
amazing it looks as good as she does I reckon
needs a fair clean out and a lick of paint
but all things considered it's held up all right
how long since anyone was here did ye say Callum
livin' on the place I mean

they were still here when you was across the river weren't they
Callum thought for a moment as he sat down on the second top step
leant back with his elbows on the veranda boards
from there he faced down across the river
over towards his family's old place
though too far away to make out specifics
too far to see more than memories

he sighed and thought slowly
that life across the river
that huge part of his life
so very far away from him now
be ten and maybe even twelve years I figure
they started being hardly ever here when Amy their little girl
when Amy got real crook

always in either Sydney or Adelaide with her
then when she passed away
I just don't think they could face the place any more
got a manager in
yeah ten years ago or so at least I reckon
no one living here properly
whoever worked it just staying where we are down at the quarters

with disapproval clear in his voice
Sid began
well there's a lot of that happenin' I can tell ye
lots of places out here are company owned
one manager
blokes like me often taking care of a few places too
it's doable I guess but not the same as having someone here doin' it proper

well there'll be someone here now Sid Harry put in
this fella's never gunna leave as I figure it
Arthur's here for the long haul don't ye reckon Callum
yeah you'll be takin' him out in a box Callum agreed
but hopefully not before he fixes the joint up a bit
then as a sudden kind of instruction to all Arthur announced
well come on then let's get on with it

heading off back in the direction of the shearers' quarters
Arthur half turned back as he walked
moving with unusual haste
the rain's stopped
a little bemused the others watched
watched this fellow with purpose
stride back across to the other buildings

Callum finally spoke the thoughts of all
I think he's half serious you know
come on then
they followed somewhat reluctantly
leaving the sparse but comfortable outlook of the wide front veranda
there'd better be a beer in it
it's definitely beer o'clock suggested Sid

they trudged across the saturated soft soil
fine ochre dust turned to a slippery greasy affair
Uncle Cecil watched the party file back from his perch
his seat on the edge of veranda outside his room
resting in full sunshine
enjoying the heat of it after the extended rain
unmoved for the two hours or so they had been gone

Arthur waved across to him from the shelter's other end
he stepped up into the kitchen and shouted
breaking the elderly man's moments of quiet and peace
do you want a cuppa or something
the others are coming back now too
I can see that answered Cecil
no I'm okay thanks all the same eh

Arthur grabbed some old dry newspaper from the pile near the pantry
went out to begin fiddling with the saturated fireplace
the others returned and began to sit around
Callum went in to the coolroom and emerged with a six-pack of beer
joining the others in an arc of various chairs
around the still unlit fireplace he announced
I declare this planning department meeting open and thus distributed the beers

as he attempted to light the fire in the wet drum
battling with dry paper and damp kindling
Arthur again called across to Uncle Cecil
asking him to join them
naaa don't drink me
no friend of drink me
and I can hear your stories from here just the same

Harry could see the disappointment or unease this stirred in Arthur
so quickly reassured
it's good mate
don't worry about Uncy there
he'll swing in when he's ready
it's fine
he'll be fine back there smokin' away and Colin's gunna stick with him look

sensing that the men were going to be just drinking and talking for a while
the young boy had left his father's side
lay across an old timber bench seat near Uncle Cecil
hard up against the wall
just in shadow of the now very warm sun
his light limbs seemed perfectly comfortable on the hard and dusty surface
so close to his special old uncle

Callum put his beer down on the ground
fossicked through the pile of timber to the side for the driest of the damp pieces
suggesting to Arthur
we can throw some diesel on it if it won't get going
Arthur was diligently blowing and fanning the humble glow
the spark he had initiated at the centre of the metal half drum
might get there without it yet he suggested hopefully

there's half a tree in old newspaper in here once it sparks up
at which Sid felt the need to contribute
she'll be right
you've got space underneath it which is the thing
it'll all be dry enough soon just see
Harry contentedly sat back in his canvas camping chair
opened a can of beer

he quietly watched the firestarters work away
enjoyed their success before asking in his open but matter-of-fact way
so Arthur
what's the master plan
and what's step one eh
though there was a chair provided for him at the centre of the crescent
Arthur was happy to stand for a while poking and encouraging the fire

he held a fresh can of cold beer in his left hand
thinking for a moment
becoming a little more used to the eyes of all upon him
well there's a bit of scope you could say
and I think I probably know more about what I don't want to do
ye know
more than what I definitely do want I reckon

how's that then Harry pursued
well I don't want goats and pigs tearing the place up
nor sheep and cattle for that matter
Arthur would have continued but for Callum's delight getting the better of him
that's it
spot on Arthur
thus prompting Sid to voice his gut reaction too

and apart from pleasing the bloody greenies like Callum here
exactly what is that gunna achieve
not running cattle or sheep
get rid of the ferals or have a go at least yeah good but whata ya plan on livin' off
I mean there's not a lot a cash in saltbush y'know mate
and I don't care how much money ye got in kitty
everything runs out in time unless there's somethin' comin' in

to which Callum jumped in before Arthur had a chance to respond
the place needs to recover first Sid
it's been flogged for years
especially the last few through this long dry stretch
it'll support nothin' if it isn't given a proper spell
then reused differently somehow
you've seen enough to know that I reckon

Arthur was surprised by two such immediate and passionate responses
felt that he should jump back in
before the argument got totally out of his hands
all I'm saying is that I wanna take it steady
work out what the place will support he began as the others listened
maybe it won't all be about saltbush and roos
maybe it could cope with a few cattle or whatever

now that's soundin' good Arty Harry threw in
it'd be a shame if there weren't just a few juicy steaks walkin' about
the laughter of all diffused the mood
something Harry so often deftly achieved
allowing Arthur to more confidently resume
I guess Sid what I'm saying what I've been thinking about so far
is pretty simple in my mind anyways

and I don't know that I'm a greenie or whatever
but what seems clear is that the place needs a break
a clear break from the things that have got it to this point
I'm also gunna need heaps of help whatever way it goes
so I reckon I also need to think about that
about the best ways to create some real jobs on the joint for some people out here
good work for people if I can swing it

now ye talkin' cuz
now ye talkin Harry exclaimed in his quiet but so sincere way
that'd be good that there ye said it right there
especially our young people eh
this welfare this sit-down-money
I ain't never seen it make someone happy yet
jobs is the thing Arty ye right there

Callum and Harry were quietly nodding approvals across to each other
their hopes for some good to flow from this strange decent fellow realised already
Sid had not lifted his gaze from the gradually establishing flames
what he had listened to had not angered him
but he figured that the intent of his invitation there from Callum
to meet this unlikely millionaire
was to give an opinion and some practical advice

Sid had been doing that most of his life
one way or another
a kind of sieve of reality
through which all kinds of nonsense schemes and ideas had filtered
just now and then a fresh chunk of worth was caught
and he sensed that somewhere in this Arthur fella
something good and practical lurked

he didn't know what it was going to be
but at least he had the essential ingredients
openness and sincerity
qualities often sadly lacking
in Sid's experience
in many people
including those with money

whatever the failings and naivety
he sensed that Arthur at least had these fundamentals
so he could potentially work with him
but Sid needed as always to get back to practicalities
and so what work would that be
if it's not gunna be sheep I mean
all eyes again towards the new owner of that large piece of land

the swift clarity of Arthur's response surprising all
this fellow so new had at least been listening and thinking things through
well
fencing's as far as I've thought just yet
but when ye look at it
just the boundary would keep a team or two going for a while
how many miles in it all up about do you reckon

the question was to all but all looked to Callum
already looking upwards
fingers fidgeting with some kind of calculator or abacus in the air
happily working on a figure he knew would be large
dozens just the bare boundary
Callum suggested in time
but some of it might not need totally redoing either

none of it would be pig and goat proof though answered Arthur
at which Sid sat up straighter in his chair
Harry looked across to the new legal landholder as he laughed
held up his beer in cheers
here's to ye cuz
ye don't plan on doin' things by halves eh
that does sound like the fence to build

Sid agreed
now that would keep a couple of teams busy for a while
there's a fact
and important work too
Sid quietly attempting some calculations of his own
before continuing
and ye know what ye could do at the same time or first up maybe

put in one or two internal paddocks
a hundred acres each say
hot-wired to fill up with wild goats gradually
I've seen a couple a fellas do it really well out this way
just a regular fence
but then with one or two electric wires all the way around
they had them pretty well contained

and goats
Christ goats are not an easy thing to fence in
yeah that's the go Harry agreed knowingly
I went to a big block a year or two back now I guess
this fella was right into that
out on the way to Tibooburra from memory
big place too

two hundred thousand or so
and anyway yeah this one paddock he set up with power all the way around
clean too them goats had fairly stripped it bare
chalk and cheese it was
between where the goats were and the paddock beside 'em
and he reckoned he sent off a semi load about every six months
would that be right Sid

clearly warming to the whole idea Sid replied
could be yeah depending on the block and the season
and the prices vary
like everything a course
but ye could be clearing thirty grand right there
with one truck load
used to be only pet food but there's a big market now

Middle East and Indonesia is the go now I think
ye could do up a couple of wired paddocks here I'm thinkin
Callum also keen to agree with Sid
sounds all right to me Arthur
getting rid of part of the problem
having some income thrown in
pay some of those wages

a moment of silence from all
disrupted by the quiet Uncle Cecil
calling from back at the end of the veranda
Mutawintji
maybe mention Mutawintji Harry
say what there Uncy called back the younger man
you tellin' me you can hear us way back there old man

Uncle Cecil snapped back
I tell ye I got many failin's
but hearing it ain't one boy
hearin' ain't one
and I sayin' tell Arthur there about Mutawintji
how it looks now
after what we been doin' up there these few years eh

well yeah that's a point all right Uncy
that's it ain't it Harry agreed
he turned back around to face the fire and the crew
thinking about what Uncle Cecil had said and how he could explain it best
Mutawintji he began before collecting his thoughts some more
a bit special
a special place all right

what Uncy there is saying is that it's a good example maybe
of what you might be able to do here eh
Harry half-turned back towards Uncle Cecil and shouted
you'll let me know if I get any of this wrong now won't ye Uncy
the older man swiftly responding to the smiles of all
oh you be hearin' from me if that be the case boy
you be hearin' from me

and so Harry proceeded
the thing is
that property there
Mutawintji
been a national park now for what
couple a decades now I guess
so it's been locked up pretty well

it's a special place all right
about halfway between Wilcannia there and Broken Hill and a bit north
always was special
not only Paarkintji
but other mobs too
kind of a shared special ground
full of paintings up in all the caves and carvings

even found some old campsites
ovens in the ground ye can see the scorched earth yet
anyhow
a few years back
Uncle Cecil's generation
back when it was still being worked as a farm
there were rumours and all sorts of worries

some of the carvings were being chipped up
sent off to Sydney to be sold
stuff like that
well these old fellas locked the place up
true
they camped up at the gate there
locked it all up

said that this is no good
we want this place back
we gotta preserve it
a special place
so anyway
the long and the short of it was
they got their way

Harry called across to Uncle Cecil without turning his way
how I doin' so far Uncy
not bad boy not bad
I taught you okay I figure came the dry reply
so anyways Harry continued
how that all came to be
well that's a whole separate story

but why Uncy mentioned it now maybe
is that they decided there early on to take all the stock off
try to get rid of all the ferals
lots of fencing and trapping and shooting
but it's heaps better now
the damage them goats especially did up in the caves and overhangs
something to see

even after all these years they haven't got rid of them entirely
but it looks heaps better now eh
Uncy and I were over that way a few months back
a bit of a big meeting about some stuff
and the place was green
at least compared to everything else
green eh

all that dry time we've had all around
they reckon they had just a few showers there
about a week before we went through
and the place had just lifted
lovely it was
but then drivin' out the place right next door
and all around dust and more dust

all around where they're still flogging the land with sheep and cattle
goats it seems unchecked
not to mention the pigs too
and they would've had the same few mills of rain I'm thinkin
same maybe as Mutawintji
one side of their good fence green
the other dry

Sid now put in
that's somethin' ye have goin' for ye here too Arthur
you've got a bit of high stuff to catch any rain that's around
that reservoir up there
mightn't seem so much
but when you get up there
it's pretty obviously the highest bit of ground around

and all that matters
they're cloud catchers those bits of hills out here
for a moment they were all content to be quiet and still
the fire building before them as the afternoon began
various words and ideas
the faint trail of Uncle Cecil's cigarette smoke
wafting over them

Arthur was prompted to reach for his tobacco pouch
Callum went to the cool room for more beers
speaking of that reservoir Arthur asked to Harry
have you thought any more on what might happen up there
well came the reply
I need to speak with Uncy more
about the protocols of it all

but I'm thinkin' that once it dries out a bit
we'll go and get the Land Council together for a meeting first
see what happens from there
I'm gunna get hold of the National Parks mob too
see if they haven't got contacts with some museum people
someone who knows all about how to preserve what's there
need to think things through

it might just dry out and all will be okay
but I dunno
I'm worried it's all gunna just crumble in a heap if it dries out real quick
this big dump of rain might be good for it but I dunno
Harry watched Arthur look at the fire
clearly pondering a few things
several things perhaps plaguing his mind

don't worry just yet mate
we won't boot ye off just yet he said with a cheeky smile
Arthur laughed a little at this as the big and clever man continued in softer tones
I've got a feeling that Uncy back over there thinks that you're okay
which is a good thing 'cause otherwise he and few of his crew
might lob up and lock the gates eh
no pressure mind no pressure

16

the drinking ceased early the following morning
only when the last of it was gone
Arthur didn't recall climbing into his single stretcher bed
headache and the furry mouth upon waking
familiar things
bugger it
said softly to himself

he attempted to rouse amid the self-inflicted nausea
the promise
to himself and a list of others
stop drinking
indeed a feeble thing
and in the haze of the really bad hangovers such as now
it was always Beth his Beth who came back to him

her calm face would be there upon waking
then as he closed eyes again tight
an attempt to recapture some kind of calm
shut out the beautiful troubling image
her face would swarm him with its gentle patient understanding
before turning into a worried frown
squeezing out a visible tear

Beth
Beth
he spoke softly to the mid-morning light
shafts poked through the window and surrounding gaps within his single room
he curled up tight in his sleeping bag
done again
done again

it wasn't the nausea that sickened him
angered him
it was his weakness
pathetic
he mouthed to the room's dusty light
stretched and slowly sat up on the floppy old squeaky old bed
metal and wire mesh

pathetic did he feel and poorly did he view himself
surely he had plumbed the depths far enough
his self-abuse now a thing inexcusable
unforgivable
considering the opportunities that fate had provided for him
from a chance good deed
great wealth had come

then consequently
during rambling yet searching journeys
he had happened upon Callum
a good man
and from that friendship
a reason to visit this open and endless country
a place of perhaps peace and opportunity to create a home

maybe also an opportunity
improve or restore the land
help some others too
if some good work could be created
and there he sat
sick and feeling weak amongst all these possibilities
how many hours of another day already wasted

reaching for his pouch of tobacco
footsteps scuffed the dusty concrete outside his door and stopped
the loud knock and booming voice belonged to Harry
wakey wakey your highness
there's a brew of tea on the go for all who are capable
Harry didn't wait for a reply from inside
and none came

there was though a smirk and a smile from Arthur
thank god for Harry he thought as he stood to rejoin the world
surprised to see that everyone else was already up and around the fire
noises of morning hadn't reached his slumber
all were eating toast
bread browned over the coals from the fire of the night that had gone
little Colin came straight up to him

offering two pieces on a plate smothered in butter and honey
it smelt wonderful
but Arthur knew he would not be able to consume it there and then
thanks mate he said to the smiling Colin
taking it from him gingerly
placing it down
maybe after a cup of tea eh

looking a little crestfallen the boy returned to the side of his father
Harry's got some news for ye Arthur
announced Callum as he slotted his bleary-eyed friend a mug of tea
top night last night eh
I don't think I've seen you drink so much since Japan
between you and Sid over there
that bottle of rum didn't stand a chance

mornin' Arthur
Sid softly acknowledged him
offering a wry smile
Arthur sheepishly sat down
content with his cigarette and large mug of tea
expecting at any time
some kind of embarrassing tale about the night before

you'd be feeling pretty good though wouldn't ye Arthur
Harry announced cheekily
having given up the grog and all
like you were saying the other day
ye'd be feelin' as fresh and sober as Uncy over there I'm thinkin'
all chuckled at Arthur's expense
he held up his mug in cheers

yep thank you thank you
I feel so much better now that I do not touch a drop
replied Arthur to perhaps sympathetic applause
well there'll be nothing to temp you tonight old son
Harry continued *that rum was the last of what's here*
oh Arthur replied and sat for a moment
quietly concerned

even though he knew he didn't need another drop
not for as long as he lived
he would love a cold can of beer right there and then
settle his stomach and perhaps his nerves
was that the news Callum said you had then
Harry laughed and continued *no no*
news is that I have to get goin'

at least I have to try to get out of here
we were talkin' just now about the others tagging along
Arthur's quizzical face clearly needed much more explanation
Harry backtracked a little before proceeding
ye see I went for a walk early like I do
don't know why but I get up early me and off
even after a big drink like last night

and anyhow I wanted to check me phone
check in to work and that there
I figured like Sid was sayin' yesterday
the highest place
somewhere I might get service would be up at that old reservoir
and bingo straight up
clear as a bell

but there was a message for me about a job I gotta get to
no power and their generator's packed it in too
just the other side of Tilpa there
so anyhow when I called them they reckon I might get through
Arthur thought on this and asked
so you all heading in then
what about those fines for driving on the roads in the wet

didn't you say it was a thousand dollars per wheel or something
yeah true true Harry explained
but I can be exempt because it's work
an emergency
and the rest of 'em following well
that'd be good seein' as I've got Colin and Uncy here with me eh
makes sense to stay together

and don't ye reckon Sid observed
that running out of grog isn't a bit of an emergency anyway
creating laughs from all
so Arthur asked Harry
stay or go cause the train's departing
Arthur struggled with being upright that morning let alone think and decide
how long will you be gone for he asked as he pondered

could be gone for a long while maybe not
depends what I find when I get to the job
if the road's okay and that river don't pop its banks
the others should be back this arvo eh concluded Harry
followed by a challenging smile to Callum
unless they get stuck at the pub
which has happened before

Arthur thought for a moment about going with them all
but his lethargy got the better of him
mate I think a few more hours sleep is all I'm good for today
thanks anyway
I'll just poke along here
but do you really think you'll get through
it seemed like we had a heap of rain

well I'm hoping that the sun yesterday and today has helped
might've put just enough cake on it
and there's a long rocky section down the way too
so we might be okay
keep an eye on the river though
that's what'll bring us unstuck
there was a fair bit due to come down and it's touch and go now

but that's okay
we'll see what happens eh
hooroo then
within a few minutes the two vehicles departed
everyone had disappeared
Arthur took his mug of tea back to his room
an attempt to chase sleep some more

at first he met with success
then the face of Beth returned
sleep came in snatches
just a few minutes at a time before waking
waking with the smiling but worried face of Beth his wife before him
finally he looked at his watch
but in the poor light of the shrouded single room couldn't make out the time

his watch the first real treat
a first purchase after his lottery win
a slightly expensive and chunky thing
he took it off
rolling the cool weight of it loosely around his hand
the watch and his leather hiking boots bought on the same day
the day his money came through

Arthur remembered sitting on his soft bed in the Plaza Hotel
putting on the boots
feeling much taller as he stood on the thick carpet
looking at himself in the long mirror
reflected behind him also the sunny beach view
he remembered looking at himself and feeling good
sensed that he was going to start afresh

set out to explore the world
and to an extent he had too
not all over as his initial imaginings had been
his funds would have certainly allowed
but for as far and as long as had made sense to him
firstly the long train up north
then the plane hop across to Papua New Guinea

there he met the crazy but very kind Hiroyuki
whose invitation he followed to Japan
that introduced him to Callum and his American mate Sam
whom he joined on their trip through China
by that time he had had enough of the travel thing
there was a fine line it seemed to Arthur
between exploration and indulgence

he did not want to become one of the several he had seen
an endlessly moving
rootless surveyor of the world
with lots of tales to tell
through somehow hollow eyes
yet no claim at all to any contribution being made
no energy put into change

after several months without a home
and the urge within him growing to do something
to settle somewhere and accomplish something
he returned to Sydney and then hooked up again with Callum at Broken Hill
then based on a good feeling and a whim
Arthur used some of his money to buy thousands of acres
dusty overworked land

well it isn't dusty any more
thought Arthur with a half smile as he emerged from the small room
searching for enough light to check the time
suspecting that perhaps the best part of the day had slipped by
robbed by his hangover slumber
three thirty and the mid-afternoon sun was warm
almost steamy with so much moisture on the ground

not the dry heat he was becoming used to
unusually muggy as he decided to walk a little in his leather hiking boots
still his comfortable trusty friends
Arthur did not need to go far before he caught a glimpse of the river
spilled over and spread out across a section of floodplain
he thought of the view from the homestead front veranda the day before
found himself running across to that same point

hot and sweating from just a little exertion
sensing on himself pouring from his skin
a kind of unpleasant beer and rum cologne
he stood in the veranda's shade
conscious of the faintest cooling breath of moving air
full on he said aloud
gazing down at the river now beyond its banks

the slow graceful arc of the river bend
now a much broader searching thing
full on he spoke again to no one
wondering what this would mean for Leopardwood
and for him
over the next few solitary days
solitary and sober days

more than loneliness
it was a kind of anxiety that visited him as the sun began to dip
he at first spent the afternoon walking through the buildings again
imagining things he would repair or improve
several times he returned to the large veranda viewing point
try to gauge if the river had continued its spread across the land
seemed not so but if still rising the river's progress was very slow

at the first sight of the afternoon fading he dined on toast
a pot of tea
retreated to his single room
a strange form of fear seemed to reach him
the thought of being the only person
amid 150,000 acres
one consideration one dull aching thought at the back of his mind

beyond that though
the notion that it was without drink that he attempted sleep
there would be no anaesthetic that evening
to dilute his demons for a while
sober but anxious
did he close his tired eyes
where perhaps Beth awaited in his dreams

17

when sleep did approach that evening
it was not his poor departed Beth who visited him
but the recent memories of Papua New Guinea
filling his half-drowsing mind
Arthur welcomed her face
looked forward to her dreamy face
yet it was more recent images that soon swirled before him

to PNG on a whim soon after his lottery luck
a starting point as good as any
hopefully leading him to the next thing
an old friend of his father's he presumed still to be there
an excuse for entering a land so enticingly different to his own
travel something that he could suddenly afford
bought him time to consider what he actually wanted to do

faces of friendships briefly formed returned so clearly in his slumber
one day in particular that would long live in Arthur's memory
even in his uneasy dreams
I hope you've got a couple of quiet ones
Arthur asked Joel the young station manager
it's been a few years since I rode
never was real flash

Joel mockingly looked him up and down
but you've got the bandy legs the cowboy legs there look
Arthur took his nervous cowboy legs over to the main house
dressed in his only pair of jeans
a cotton shirt that still felt stiff and new
boots were made for hiking not galloping through scrub
trying to poke through the jungles of PNG

he altogether felt like the out-of-place new boy
breakfast smells hit him before he even reached the lush garden
bacon sausages steak and eggs
the ageing servant
a dignified man perhaps in his seventies
again busily catering for all
shuffled a plate before the new boy as he sat down

Arthur ate with Joel until Kevin soon emerged
and how are the cowboys this morning he beamed
this diesel mechanic the only other non-PNG fella on the property
for the few days Arthur was there
Kevin wearing the same clothes as the night before
thickets of hair from a bulky torso escaped the greasy singlet everywhere
are you riding in that asked Arthur innocently

riding the large man choke-screamed his reply
you must be bloody joking
the offer is always there Kev Joel chimed in
yeah well the offer can bloody well stay right there
be buggered
let the cowboys do their job and let me do mine that's all
and he settled in to his meal

several young men waited with the horses outside
Joel introduced Arthur to all in Pidgin
triggering lots of smiles and a murmur of chuckles
two of the crew came over to shake hands
Joel explained to Arthur that he would ride with them
Henry and Smacka looked like the business all right
Arthur sensed a wave of both excitement and fear

warm betelnut red smiles and soft handshakes
lean chiselled black arms welcomed him
Smacka handed over the reins to a lovely-looking chestnut mare
both men spoke to him in their tongue quickly
to each other gesticulated wide and far
Arthur nodded and smiled
the vacant hopeful smile of a foreigner lost

Joel saw him struggling and so moved nearby on his speckled mount
you'll be right
just follow them
Arthur again looked his guides and tutors up and down
both wearing tight blue jeans
bare-footed and cotton business shirts tucked in
sleeves and collars removed

they nodded to each other and to Arthur then remounted
clearly keen to get started now
only two things to remember Joel suggested
Arthur looked and strained to listen as he steadily moved away
any advice from Joel would be something upon which to rely
what colour is Henry's shirt Arthur
red he replied a little bemused

and Smacka's Joel smiled *is blue*
there are two colours to remember and that is all
just follow
Arthur still did not look too amused as Joel continued
you'll be okay
you can't get too lost anyway
the river runs right through this place

we're heading downstream now to push them back up
only need ten good steers for the cool room
see you back up at the yards
anything I need to know about the horse the visitor asked
no
she's a lovely old thing replied Joel swiftly
I used to ride her a lot when I first got here

they've looked after you
she's a real quiet one
Arthur checked the tightness of the saddle
placed a hand on the animal's warm neck
what's her name
Joel thought and then smiled
her name I guess is the chestnut mare

Arthur got himself in the saddle
as smoothly as he could remember or dare
hiking boots feeling awkward
almost tight in the light metal of the stirrups
but he was there
soon very clear that at least the horse knew what was expected that day
following red and blue at a canter and they were on their way

the cleared country continued beyond Arthur's expectations
well beyond the homestead surrounds
what he could recall from the small plane dropping down from the clouds
looking down upon dense lush moss it seemed
the jungle canopy viewed from above
yet stray away from the main part of the valley floor
the real vegetation soon had the upper hand

even throughout the valley cleared there were pockets
dense pockets here and there
by the river larger trees
the stilted dwellings of a village casually entered
horses had followed the river for quite a time
before reaching the packed earth of well-worn paths
a village entered

courtyards of dirt irregular though logical and balanced somehow
muddy pools from the downpour the day before
fringes also almost dust so soon
a large sow and five piglets
turned their ambling into a trot upon realising horses and men
then just beyond the elevated and fragile structures of timber and straw
three steers grazed a lush patch of green

they startled quickly
Arthur watched in awe at his mounted companions
each steer somehow punched a hole through the nearest dense wall of green
red and blue following straight in behind
the controlled sedateness of the ride thus far instantly gone
in a moment Arthur felt totally out of his league
he wouldn't lead in let alone push a horse through there

but it was all he could do to stop the chestnut mare
clearly not fazed by launching into green
with or without a hesitant rider
reluctantly it obeyed Arthur's reins
instead the two skirted the edge of darkness
horse and rider peering with equal concern
for signs of the horses or two colours amid the shadows deep

Arthur even flirted with the thought of diving in
if he could even get some glimpse of light through it all
but none emerged
so he stayed within the known world
straining to see movement or colour
then after some uncertain moments
he stopped the mare to listen

hoping for some bellowing cattle
perhaps the hollers of Henry and Smacka
but the only thing in his sphere was the mare's snorting breath
then cicadas
waves of cicadas rolling through the trees
each time their drill momentarily abated
silence was filled by the sound of the large swift flowing stream

the mare stepped with care down a soft track to the cooling water
choosing an almost still pool
water eddying back around
below some large boulders worn smooth
Arthur's mare drank
nuzzled into the purling cool
pulling reins from the rider's loose hands

Arthur felt an immediate unease
nothing in his hands
no means of even partial control
edge of the saddle or a handful of coarse mane
no compensation for those strips of leather now just beyond him
the horse bent its head low
enjoying the water and the cool

reins wet in the water
snaking above the surface and below
their leather a darker colour suddenly
flicked from the rider's hand
anxious warm hands
into a cool clear flowing mountain stream
dunked again each time the mare chose to drink some more

after several long minutes of cooling calm for the mare
high anxiety for the fretful rider
the two emerged from the stream
Arthur leaning full forward
grasping a mane as the horse carefree
bounded with grace up onto a soft grass level bank in shade
and there she stood

awaiting instruction
yet reluctant to give up the reins
each time Arthur leant forward to reclaim them
she would pull more swiftly away
and so they stood
horse sweat and wet leather
filling the thick humid air

with no alternative but to dismount
Arthur eased his large right boot from its stirrup too tight
attempting to calmly yet swiftly swing down
vulnerably he stood beside the mare
both aware of the balance of power
a hand stroking the neck and mane hopefully
as she passively allowed the poor rider to grab reins and scramble back on board

though greatly relieved
he wondered how he could be useful now
deciding the best thing to do for Red and Blue
was to not get miserable and lost
and so he turned to retrace as well as he could
the circuitous and now lonely path
unsure why the mare had not bolted and left him there on foot fragile

the mare now happily carrying the coward upon her back towards home
the return leg of an unknown journey was often a strange thing
Arthur had observed
perhaps it was to do with the uncertainty of destination
that made the journey out longer somehow
longer than the stretch heading home
but this ride back was not so

this ride led to more anxiety at every turn
should he trust the mare to take the shortest course
should he attempt to replay the landmarks in reverse
it in fact became a little of both
Arthur loosening his reins to trust the mare when he lost his way
and as the path was remembered at times
attempted to regain control

this uncertainty and the constant hope
of spotting a red or blue flash
made for a lengthy and fretful return
finally he sighted a familiar cluster of buildings
then up ahead some stockmen
possibly Joel pushing a mob
twenty or so large Brahman steers

still no colours worried Arthur to himself
as just then a lone beast burst out of the thicket beside him
the mare startled at first then clicked into gear
cutting off the run of the beast already stressed tired and confused
then behind him jumped Henry and Smacka
red and blue
pursuing still the other befuddled steers

seeing Arthur they waved and cheered him on
lifting entirely the foreigner's mood
once spotted their three joined up with the main mob
and soon all were funnelled along the fence line
up into the yards
a restless angry loud twenty-four-strong herd
agitated by their new confines

Arthur dismounted elated
sweating through his shirt and moist new jeans
he patted the neck and shoulders of his new friend
the very patient chestnut mare
it sniffed at the air and Arthur's proximity
Henry and Smacka approached him hurriedly
beaming and together shaking his hands

good good very good they said together and then separately
Joel came over smiling to pass a large water bottle around
seems like you did okay
to which Arthur could only laugh and shake his head
looking down and around at the swirl of stockmen who were real
those fellas are cowboys all right Joel
you should have seen where they rode

a fire was lit and a large hotplate upon it
the elderly cook from the house already there and prepared
shifted around deftly large portions of steak
a little grim thought Arthur
to taunt the still living beast in the yard just metres away
but the smell was sensational and everyone's mood was high
not least Arthur who felt suddenly and pleasantly part of a team

he stood near the fire
odd he thought the attraction of embers
as hot and sticky as the day was
he and the others all seemed drawn to it still
the last thing needed was more heat
yet it was a simple pleasure
a focal point that could be watched over forever

a fire
a new baby
perhaps the sea
things to gaze upon with wonder
without tiring
stockmen chatted in the one large circle
of which Arthur was included

through their laughter and mimicry
even the newcomer enjoyed the replaying of the ride
for the mute Arthur
ignorant of their tongue
banter was a wonderful melody accompanying the scene
occasionally amid chuckles
Red or Blue would hold his hand as men there do

slap him on the shoulder and laugh again with the team
rough meat seared was soon consumed
a large slab of soft white bread thrust into each hand
a slightly larger cut of meat
heat reaching through the slice of bread to Arthur's soft white hands
mugs of tea strong sweet black tea
tobacco smoke swirling through the campfire air

a young woman stood holding a small baby on the opposite side of the yards
Joel approached her and they spoke briefly
matter-of-factly
yet all the while his hand touched the head of the babe
he spotted Arthur and waved him around
Arthur I have some things to do with these cattle
this is my wife and he was gone

I'm Arthur he said awkwardly
presuming but not sure that she would understand him
hello was the soft reply
my name is Lila and this
she unwrapped her bundle a little
this is Samuel
speaking with the tired calm of a baby's mother

he is now ten weeks old
Arthur watched Lila as she rearranged her load
tightening the large string bag with a single knot
ensuring that little Samuel was asleep and enclosed
these bags are something aren't they
the way they can be used for everything it seems
Arthur observed

bilum she smiled
oh yes bilum is very good
but this little man is getting heavy just the same
the indigo and green string fibre bag stretching
arcing around her treasure like a weighty cocoon
where was Samuel born asked Arthur
is there a hospital near here

Lila looked at him and slightly frowned
no
no doctor here
I am from Poppandetta and so we wanted to be there
near my family
Joel's family are from near there on the north coast too
so close to my time Mr Jackson he called for the plane

but the plane didn't come before my baby
we were waiting by the strip
but Joel and I had to go just over there
you see those trees
between the stockyard and the grass airstrip
perhaps five hundred metres away
a clumsy collection of small trees

it was very hot but we had some shade there
concluded the calm young mother
Jesus wept gasped Arthur
were you scared
Lila paused
yes of course yes of course
a first baby for me and for Joel

we were scared
and no family to help
all far away
just lucky
very lucky Mr Kevin was there
Arthur's face must have betrayed his surprise
Lila smiled up at him and nodded assuredly

oh yes Mr Kevin was there and it was all okay
he calmed Joel and me
he says he has seen many babies
yes we had to have our Samuel just there
waiting for that plane
but he is good now and next week we go to Poppandetta to my family
that will be very nice

Arthur looked many times at those trees
then back to Lila and the perfect little boy she held
fearing what may have been
trying to imagine Kevin's big diesel paws
delicately holding up new life
possibly helping Joel to cut the cord
Arthur looked at her looking at the sleeping child

18

Frank extended his telescopic arm across the bar
delivering three more beers
what about your boy and Uncy over there Harry he asked
Harry about to pay for the round
yeah same again for them too then
lemonade or whatever they had eh he replied
distributing beers along to Sid and Callum

Frank took two more cold cans and glasses full of ice across to a corner table
Uncle Cecil smoked
leaning back against the wall
barely awake
the boy beside him already in and out of slumber
crouched over the table
his head resting on slim tired forearms

here you go then
the tall wiry middle-aged publican plonked the cool objects down
near the edge of the round table
just inches from the face of the boy
a thick glass ashtray lay just beyond the new objects
the new things dewy as they melted into the warm dry air
Colin looked at the beading cans

his head comfortable finally
resting to the side on the table
the rickety table that moved each time Uncle Cecil stubbed out a cigarette
through a tall schooner glass filled with ice
the boy saw parts of the crazy lanky thin shape of Frank the publican
move away back towards the bar distorted
the man was a funny shape anyway Colin figured

he wondered if the narrow shoulders and long neck stooped always
or was it just when he was in that low-roofed bar
serving beers and other things to all the grown-ups
mostly men who drank and then got all loud and silly
who drank so that they could get silly
sometimes start into fighting
Colin didn't like it when silly turned to loud and then became fighting

Frank had soon moved
beyond the tight funny hemisphere of Colin's glass
resuming his place at the bar opposite Harry and his friends
the boy picked up the glass full of ice
he could look at someone else
anything else he chose
through a different lens

the open rectangular doorway near his table and the trees beyond
all went wonky
bent as the glass was raised up close to his eyes
timber and glass doors led out onto the scruffy courtyard
the bank with the full flowing river behind
he turned his toy onto Uncle Cecil
just as a spidery hand rose up to position a smoke

one more cigarette rolled
placed between smooth and weathered lips
despite eyelids looking heavy with sleep
the shape the glass created of his Uncle made the boy laugh
and the old man too
once he saw what the child was up to
the older moved his head from side to side while smiling

a silly broad smile to make the boy laugh even more
Colin scanned the room in a slow arc
the glass moist in his hand
ice swishing around more easily as it began to melt into its surrounds
the backs of three men at the bar
his dad then Callum and Sid
all fatter through his funny ice goggles

his dad and Sid were big men anyway
now just wider still
it was the slim and fit-looking Callum who made the boy laugh out loud
suddenly appearing chubby and middle-aged
Frank's wife
a short strong-looking woman
flecks of grey in her short-cropped hair

stouter still as she bent and rattled trays
glasses in and out of the steaming dishwasher
objects behind the bar
bottles and glasses of various colour and size
distorted bulbous flashes to Colin
he toured the room with his new eyes
coming to rest on a section of the written walls

walls and the ceiling
every possible inch of the place
bore the signatures of drinkers and travellers who had visited before
a donation to the Royal Flying Doctors the fee requested
a signed guarantee of immortality inside the Tilpa Hotel
some signatures were scrawled
too strange for him to read

even when he took the schooner glass away from his eyes
attempting to read them properly
and a good reader he was despite his years
his mum and dad never happier it seemed
than when they sat with him
in bed or on their floppy old lounge
listening to their son mouth the words from one of his favourite books

he enjoyed trying to figure the new words out
mum or dad patiently pointing and correcting him
there were plenty of new things to challenge on the walls in the pub
he mouthed the possibilities aloud
Ma...vis...Keeley... Eliz...abeth...someone... Thomas...Huxley...
Colin played with the letters for a while
moving the moistening glass before his eyes

then he decided to just read them
as many as he could
sipping some melted ice
holding the cool thing to his bony chest
then up to his forehead and face in damp pats as he chose
the words amused him
he read the names as he thought they would be pronounced

imagining faces
sometimes the stature that each signature conjured
Winsome and Hank...Sally Frankston...Arthur...somebody...hey Dad
there's an Arthur name here
is it Arthur
it must be our new friend Arthur
eh Dad

just a minute
we're talkin here boy
Harry said quietly but firmly as he brought his son in closer
under his arm
as he listened to Frank's talk of the rain up north
what he had heard was going to make its way down
weather talk and maybes

when the speaking stopped the boy became shy again
the men all looked to him
snuggling now beneath the bulk of his father
now boy
his father encouraged him
tell us again what you found
and so the boy pointed to where he had just been

just there Dad
Arthur's written his name
Harry smiled at his boy
true
well he didn't mess around did he
I been here all me life
don't know that I've got around to it yet

the other men laughed with Harry
Frank bent down from across the counter to speak to Colin
you're right Colin
Arthur did write his name
but not that one there
they're all old ones there
come over here with me and see if we can't find him proper eh

Colin left his father's side
the large glass still grasped in his slim hand
followed Frank across the room
they scanned the corner walls for a moment
looking for the one name to pop out from amongst the cluttered scrawl
the marks of so many passing lives
there look

Colin pointed up a little higher than he could reach
Frank scanned across and down
confirmed with a smile and patting the boy on his slight shoulders
perhaps a little too hard
that's him
that's him all right
well done son

well spotted
just the other week Arthur put that up there
when he first came in with Callum
Frank returned to the bar while Colin continued with his reading
hopeful of another discovery
lots of these not real neat Dad
he called across more confidently

Arthur too and lots of these other people
they don't write real neat
his father and the other men smiled at the young critic
he's sharp that one Harry
must be his mum's side eh
Frank concluded to the amusement of all
no arguments there mate Harry laughed

looking at his young boy
still busy scanning the walls
he's ahead of me already true
then Frank queried from his place behind the bar
punctuating Harry's wistful thoughts
so Callum
what's the go with your mate Arthur anyway

the publican's long lean frame bending down
forearms resting on the bar towels
faded cloths that ran the length of his tidy bar
Callum thought for a time
looking into the large glass of beer before him
half-empty
yeah well he's an interesting one

a bit of a unit all right is our Arthur
good bloke though
Frank pursued
cashed up is he deciding that now commenced
any conversation about this new fellow
should result in learning
discover some real information

pretty well I think Callum directly replied
grateful that neither Harry nor Sid jumped in
did not straightaway explain the extent of Arthur's means
so should I start a book on how long he'll stay
or is he a keeper ye reckon Frank asked
getting three more clean glasses
ready for the beers he expected to be requested

Callum looked across to Harry as he replied
oh I reckon he'll stay
he's still working it through in his head just how
but he wants to make a go of it eh Harry
to which Harry put in without hesitation
yeah he's the business I reckon him
he's a stayer I'm thinkin'

this sort of country's new to him right enough
but he wants to learn ye know
and he listens
at least from what I can see anyways
Sid pondered then replied
with a touch of judgement
next few days might sort him out a bit

not such an easy thing
being totally on ye Pat Malone out here as ye know
especially when ye feet have barely touched the ground
and Harry reminded
he'll be doin' it without any grog at all
but he'll be no good to you anyhow Frank
he's giving it up full stop

to which Harry broadly added with a smile
at least that's what he's said
every time I've seen him hungover
more laughter as three more beers were set up
he really does though I think Callum defended
he was even talking about cutting right down over in Japan
and that's a while ago now

barflies don't change the world
he said more than once
barflies
don't know that he wants to change the world exactly
but he does want to do something
really
he does

well said Sid knowingly
he'll have a bit of time these next few days
to get used to the idea of not drinkin'
there's nothin like a bit of enforced solitude for it
sorting things out in ye head
he's lucky but eh
all this rain straight up

how many people have bought somewhere and then bang
there's a river rise and some decent rain hits here too
struth
after all this weather even a place like Leopardwood will have feed
allowing Harry to correct him
feed for the natives only though Sid don't forget
none of ye pesky cloven-hoofed beasts over on that block mate

Callum joined Harry in the laughter
Sid clearly unamused
yeah well
that all sounds real fine
but he'll be run down with goats and pigs
unless he actually does all that fencing
gets some shooters in

irritated by the lightness of the others
yet Sid didn't want to seem angry entirely
feed their sport at his expense
it's about balance as I see it anyhow
the place has been flogged
fair enough
and that can't continue no

but to go too far the other way
not have any cattle or sheep at all
well
I just start to wonder what's the point of that at all
that's not farming to me
that's a waste of a resource if ye go that far
waste of a decent block

so is old mate a greenie then asked Frank
probably a good thing he has stopped drinkin
'cause I don't sell green beer here
Sid and Frank exchanged smirks
shook their disapproving heads
nah he just wants to fix the place up suggested Callum
or give it a chance to recover more like

always ready for a debate about the land
always ready to defend his friend
crikey Sid the place was a dustbowl
they still had it stocked right till the end
it'll take some coming back
and anyway
where's the waste in harvesting roos

why not try to make a go of that
it takes someone with cash behind them to do something different I guess
and the place might end up more productive than ever eh
Sid considered for a moment
responded
well
I'm happy to give him a hand

manage it and all that fencing for a time
if that's what he wants
speaking as if giving a speech he had thought right through
happy too to work with him
clearing out a whole bunch of ferals as well
that's always a thing worth doin'
could be a top property

given time
and the fact that he doesn't have to put beasts back on
soon as he can
like most other strugglers out here I know
and that gully up through the guts of it
then all that higher country to suck in any weather
well that's gold that is

all I'm saying is
if it starts lookin' like I think it could
and all he's doin' is growin' roos and pickin' native herbs
well
that be the end of me
dust and tail lights
I'll be out if it starts to look more like a national park than a block

exchanging understanding nods with Sid
Frank exclaimed *yeah well*
I think we've got our fill of parks haven't we already strike me
prompting Harry
beginning calmly
funny thing Callum
a big voice restrained yet ready to build

you'd think that those there carvings
all that stuff up there
you'd think that anyone seein' 'em there
would reckon they be worthy of a park
a bit of protectin' wouldn't ye say
Harry had spoken well clear enough for Sid and Frank to hear
no need for Callum to respond with Sid sure to jump back

yeah and of course it's special stuff up there Harry
ye know I don't mean it ain't
but I can't see Arthur there doin' the dirty on ye
he'll look after it as well as he can for sure I reckon
it's the rest of the place I'm gettin' at
but Sid Harry replied
his voice still an angered calm

that's all good
but what about the next one
he gathered his beer and his son
planning on some different air outside
Arthur I don't know well
but I'd trust him yeah
but he'll go one day 'cause everyone does

and then what
you or Frank here might have a big win
buy the place eh
then where would we be
where would that place
that special place that some redneck turned into a reservoir
where'd it be then eh

no offence mate
but ye don't strike me to be the caring custodian type
not exactly oozing understanding of cultural perspectives
he pushed open the ageing timber framed glass door
heading to the river right there with his son behind
ye don't know what ye don't know
none of us do

19

Arthur appeared into a crisp clear morning
having experienced a restful slumber
the sleep of a sober man
thirty-six hours or more he figured
since his last alcohol
already there were murmurings in his body
breaths of positive change

he didn't even feel like reaching for his tobacco straight away
deciding to wait and have one with a cup of tea
stepping into the kitchen
light that was handy in there no matter what time of day
did not come on
nor did the electric kettle light turn red
no power and a cool room freshly stocked with food

the diesel generator was in a small shed
just behind the shower block
his legs straddling a remaining puddle
he reached a hand through the rough-cut half-moon
a hand searching blind through the corrugated iron door
to work loose the stiff bolt latch on the inside
barely moving as he cursed and hurried yelling at the clumsy thing

*and why the hell would you want to bolt it from the inside anyhow
dumb-arse design*
then as if in retribution
the door extracted from Arthur a gash
in his haste when the stiff latch finally yielded and slid across
slit open his wrist at the base of the right thumb
the wound leaving a white leaf of lifting skin

Arthur watched it for a moment before the blood came
folding the small flap back down in place
he retrieved a less than clean handkerchief
deep in his front jeans pocket
after some juggling by his left hand
with the aid of teeth clenching a corner of the cotton square
Arthur managed to pull the temporary bandage thing tight

he could proceed with the generator
all the while angered by his stupidity
he recalled being shown to the shed
the agent that day he had decided there and then to buy Leopardwood
Arthur could picture the sales agent
a young pudgy fellow in a striped linen shirt and moleskin trousers
cleaner than he'd seen on any working farmer

explaining all quite casually
generator back-up is always there
and ample to run the whole house and all here
you've got it feeding off your main diesel tank there look
the new owner looked up at the tank
high on its metal stand beside the shed
remembering the words of the agent

seemed so long ago
though only a short time really
that day with the young agent
who backed off the hard sell as the inspection proceeded
sensing a probable sale
Arthur walked this time into the dusty space
another space entered for the first time

muddy boots slipping a little on the cement floor
he could recall nothing in the way of explanation
how to get the lump of an engine in front of him operational
a larger version of the old Lister he knew at the mill
an old faithful that powered his saw bench at the mill years before
he searched for a crank handle
could see none obviously there

all looked as though it had been quiet for years
the bank of batteries and cabling
further intimidated him with their meandering woven unexplained lines
sensing his wrist throbbing a little he lifted it up to his chest
the crude bandage now a fairly saturated untidy thing
a sensible bloke would see to that first
power may well come back on soon

once retreated to the shearers' quarters
he sought out some treatment for the wound
a painted metal first aid cupboard
attached to the kitchen wall just inside near the door
he remembered Callum opening it up the first night they were there
making some comment about how he should restock it sometime soon
Arthur was amazed that it contained anything at all

doubly grateful just then
when he actually needed it
finding for his purposes a broad bandage
some softer swaddling
an unopened if slightly old slender box
containing a tube of antiseptic cream
Arthur sat down at the kitchen table to do some repairs

re-examining the wound
he realised how close he had come to a serious problem
the gash only an inch or so long
but the blue-grey lines of arteries and veins
raised up perilously close by from his soft wrist skin
he tended the now stinging messy thing
recalling old Hank from his years at the mill

funny the things you remember thought Arthur
old Hank
who disappeared for a few days
after what was termed a mishap
Hank rarely missed a day
so when he returned after being absent for a week or so
Arthur quizzed him about what had actually occurred

his response
even so many years later remembered
still brought a chill and also a smile
oh I managed to just clip me shin with the chainsaw
that's all
still got two legs but there ye go
that's what happens when ye rush ye see son

a good thing though
a small mishap like that I reckon
yep
a good thing I always think
wakes ye up a bit see
and with any luck
the little stuff-ups stop ye having a big one see

Arthur wound the bandage as firmly and neatly as he could
around his little stuff-up
sighing with some gratitude
it would not be ideal
he pondered
marooned as he was
to slice an artery or break a bone accidentally

he left the poor light of the kitchen
checked his finished handiwork in the clear sunshine
the warmth of the sun
though not yet mid-morning the heat surprised him
he figured that if there was no spot of blood thus far
peeking through the firm bandage
he might even be able to get on and do something with the day

he sat by the cold fire a moment
enjoyed the warming of his back
strengthened by the sun
though the hand suddenly more fragile
he decided to move
once decided Arthur headed across to the homestead
the first task to be determined

cleaning out the old stone house would be a start
as good a project as any
so he figured
in any case
it had to be done sometime
so why not now while on his own
why not commence that one thing now

as he walked along the rocky slightly sloping ground
Arthur looked down across to the river
noticing that the water had not progressed at all
it had spilled across a few acres of the floodplain as supposed to do
as it had done for generations
yet perhaps not the expanse he had presumed
not what he thought he would wake to find

all was wet and there were small pools everywhere
but this was the result of the downpour
not the overflows of a river once so grand
apparently now so abused
Arthur gazed across
tried to gaze beyond his side of the Darling
tried to make out any features of what was once Callum's family property

though he stood only a little elevated
distances were vast and the horizon clear
he could see no structures nor landmarks at all
perhaps from up at the reservoir
if he looked with purpose
he might see something
Arthur thought though about Callum's brother

how an accident had got hold of him
how Callum had explained that the wind
as it blew up into a dry storm
turned an old shed door into a sail
swiftly crushed him
his brother
beloved brother

too far from care by the time the plane came
Arthur thought of all that happening just across there
across the Darling
Paarka
at a shed he'd never seen however many miles away
the death of a young man he'd never known
and he thought of Callum losing his big brother

the golden-haired child too
as Callum told it
the one who was tagged for the farm
how his parents packed up and sold it all
amid grieving for their firstborn son
still
it's easy to die anywhere Arthur murmured alone to dry air

boots crunching as they stopped on a pile of loose fine pebbles
the small collection had been pushed by the recent flow
water along the path to be caught by the accidental lie of the land
the crush of pink and yellow forms already partly dry
a little more height to see not much more
he thought again about how lucky he was to be there
or to be anywhere alive

remembered one particular beating in the park
one night that made him wonder if he would wake again
a fight between two others about what he could not recall
suddenly everyone involved
such wild days and yet even then
when he was smashed up with no home
no family any more

even then he didn't welcome death
he certainly wasn't embracing life at the time
but even so he fought to remain within its sphere
funny that
he pondered
you want to keep on living
even when you don't know what you're living for

he looked across to the old homestead
smiling at the thought that Harry would especially approve of it
that morning sitting up there looking freshly washed
sparkling in the sunshine
outbuildings too
spaced out and placed just right somehow
seemed as though they had enjoyed a drink from the lengthy storm

then he saw it
the smithy he yelled as he noticed his favourite small structure
water lapping at its doors
still above the floodplain
though clearly the lowest of all the associated buildings
the workshop sat within a kind of bowl below the others
so much water seemed to be pooling around

without the water lying as it did here and there
Arthur would have never noticed these small vagaries of the land
this one detail did distress him though
he ran straight down to the mess to see what he could save
though only a few inches deep
he could see that the water was well in under the door
worse was that more was flowing in still

a drain had coursed its way down from the main house
flowing steadily
running back up across to the shearers' quarters
he selected from Callum's veranda full of brand-new tools
a mattock and curved post hole shovel
exhausted and sweating heavily
before he even began the job at hand

but he leaned in just the same
figuring that if he could pick the lowest point
cut a channel through
he'd be able to drain the bulk of the trouble away
for thirty minutes or so he fairly went at it
worked hard at the task
sickened by his lack of either strength or stamina

the bandage on his wrist held
though he felt the wound pulsing some as he moved the sodden earth away
when he finally got a trickle moving along
along the clumsy line he had scratched
the smallest drain through the damp soil
he stood with a stiff back and sore hands
nauseous and a little light in the head

leaning back down he placed his right cheek upon the top of sweaty hands
hands cupped over the end of the mattock handle
the head of the thing stopped perpendicular to the ground
where the last necessary blow had been struck
full-on he sighed to himself while thinking
if I want to fix this place up at all
the first task will be to fix me

20

after a hopeless afternoon and night of broken sleep
Arthur rose with the first shafts of light
determined to make the most of the new day
he returned from what should have been a short task
at the smithy shed
a feeble shambles of a man
cursing grog and tobacco and the years that had intervened

after quaffing several cups of water he had made it into his single room
and there he stayed
determined to rest and awake a better specimen
the first time he stirred it was already dark
feeling as though he needed to be sick
he walked out to the veranda and the bare courtyard
bending as he stood in the dark with hands on knees

a wave of ill-health convulsed his frame
slightly relieved after this he stood and stretched back
arms and outstretched hands accidentally scanning the remarkably starlit sky
sleep came thereafter
more sound if sporadic
waking often into the darkness
he at one time tried the light switch on the wall above his bed

still nothing
still no electricity
there he was in the middle of the night
in the middle of thousands of acres
a beautiful and eerie vastness
land that he was trying to convince himself belonged to him
feeling crook and weak and alone

as the first murmur of a new day appeared
through the window and the cracks around the door
he was up and out of the small room
the bitter and furry taste in his mouth
stale tobacco
not a new sensation
though on that morning it also had the flavour of the ill

his exhaustion had both surprised and frightened him
he wondered
during some of the fragile night hours
if he were capable of good health and solid work ever again
there was so much to do that would be enjoyable and rewarding
yet his lack of capacity at the first few hurdles before him
an infuriating thing

he determined to give it a proper go
never again feel frail and helpless
a result of his own neglect and self-abuse
the road to recovery
he determined
commenced with the resurrection of the fire
a small can of beans on toast and a large mug of sweet black tea

it was the beginning already of his third straight day without grog
and just the thought of tobacco brought forth another wave of nausea
the image of him dry-reaching beneath a cool dark moon
in the middle of the night before
small steps he said to himself
but ones he was glad he had taken
sensed he was on the right track

not just with his own recovery
but also that of the property
yet he needed to take the steady and lengthy road
not go at things full-on
a bull at a gate
unthinking
impatient

his cut wrist
that near physical collapse down at the smithy shed
and for that matter the whole business up at the reservoir
all examples of how not to go about things
bull at a gate that's what you are
he could hear the voice of his Beth chastising
she would mock him and scold him and then love him still

defend her husband just the same
he had thought of her more deeply
more regularly since his lottery win
after her death and his rapid demise
he knew that he carried her with him all the time
but he also had his bundle loaded up and overflowing
with shame and self-loathing

as much as he missed her
he was also glad she was not a witness
not a witness to his despair
now though
now he had experiences and things he would have loved her to share
thinking of her brought a deep sadness
a melancholy that was hard to bare

one thing Callum said to him back in China
up in Tibet
just after Arthur had spilled his guts suddenly to he and Sam
about his years on the street and the lottery win
losing Beth
a simple thing that Callum said
something that he hung onto

and it confirmed Callum as a fellow who qualified as a good friend
I reckon Arthur
when you miss someone
and they're gone for good
it's real hard
probably always will be
but what you can do is live in a way that will honour them

it all sounds a bit grand
but if you can simply do stuff that you know they would approve of
well then
that at least makes you feel okay
practically
in practical ways
and I reckon emotionally too

though he didn't know of Callum's brother's accident at the time
Arthur now figured that it was from that experience
that heartache
from which he spoke
and he lived his words too
from what Arthur could see
Callum was determined to do something

make a difference in his own way
and in a way
Arthur suspected
that would sit well with his departed big brother
his studying
travels afar
and now returning to find his own way

all things surely
markers of a life thought through
days appreciated
objectives set
small goals realised
achievements that any older brother
might be proud

Arthur pondered his actions
his goals achieved if any
his love and his loss
Beth
Beth had not long stopped drinking and smoking
on account of her pregnancy
before she was struck by a car

just started hinting that Arthur consider the same
consider his health
their well-being
then she died
the mill unexpectedly closed
his workplace of years disappeared
and the street quite swiftly became a welcoming blur

no pressure then
to reassess your social standing
no need for a sense of self once there
just survival mode
the next drink
where to make a safe camp
life reduced to day to day

how he had traversed those times
seemed a mystery to him now
why he clung on to living
when so much of what he did was beyond care
Arthur was grateful so many times
his Beth had not seen him there then
she'd not witnessed his fall

and yet now
beneath a clear blue pale blue autumn sky
walking across to his new motorbike
ready to attempt to explore his property
most of which he had yet to see
he so wished
for an extra new helmet there

they could ride together
she could snuggle in
hold him tight from behind
as they traversed the land
their property
ride together
and realise the breeze

Arthur took a few moments to locate the gloves
he was sure Callum had also bought gloves
in his very thorough shopping spree
there'd seemed no need to wear them before
but he now had a fragile wrist that needed some protecting
the bandage looked firm and not bloodied at all
a glove would surely aid it more

gloves found amid some other clothing
things for motorbikes not yet used
the gloves some kind of synthetic fibre
firm without being too harsh
reaching up well beyond the wrist
his wound felt supported and secure
nothing to prevent his ride at all

Arthur figured that rather spending his time poking around
doing tasks that may well further aggravate his wound
the several days or however long of solitude
should perhaps be better spent getting to know his property
there was ample fuel
and if he just poked along
the bike should get him anywhere

it was the road along the river
connecting him to the outside world that was least possible
Arthur intended to just follow the fence lines
taking the basic map of the place he had with him
see what most needed repair
perhaps get a more decent feel for the place
this place he had decided would be his home

the day perfectly clear and the sun
though not containing the heat of summer
definitely beginning to dry the earth already
the mostly rocky low ridgeline
upon which the shearers' quarters
homestead and associated buildings were scattered
extended east away from the river quite some way

easy going on the bike if he took care
he and Callum had followed the southern boundary fence the other day
and so Arthur veered north to find the opposing fence line
in doing so he cut across the track out to the shearing shed
deciding to firstly revisit there
in the hope that from that central point
he could follow the wires to the northern side

the shed was three or four kilometres from the homestead
in reality nowhere near the centre of the property
but it was a focal point just the same
and for Arthur
trying to feel his way
working around the place for the first time without a guide
it was an important touchstone

the track out to it
a dusty swift ride in the new utility of the selling agent
during his first visit
now a very different thing
there was no danger of him going too fast along there that day
the first of three creeks to cross
nearly brought him to a halt straight away

water had come and gone in a hurry along them
but the soft moist soil left behind was a challenge for a less than perfect rider
he took the first one too tentatively
ended up nearly stuck entirely
not far into his journey he was already tired
reaching the large shearing shed unscathed
turned off the bike for a proper look around

he stopped close up near the metal steps
same steps the young agent had taken him to before
removing his tight helmet
the smell of the place was overwhelming
yet in a good way
mixture of moist dusty earth
sheep manure and lanolin

he peered in beneath the structure
all seemed dry
though only in there
muddy puddles large and small scattered everywhere
still with water in the high traffic areas
around the pens and at the base of stairs
but not beneath the expanse of boards

all was quiet and dry
mounds of dung accumulated
perhaps not cleaned out for years
only towards the edge of the building had the wet extended in
making a brown cake thing darker and less pleasant again
Arthur grimaced a little at the thick smell
moving quicker up the metal stairs

I'll know where to come anyhow
when I want to kickstart that rose garden
turning the latch
opening the door into the shed
was to enter a different world
boards worn smooth over time
the bale press still

quiet machinery ready in each stand
even the odd remnant of wool
on the floor and the sorting table
all had the look of being vacated only moments before
and in reality it had not been so long since the last fleece was shorn
Arthur had never been at a shed while it was working
yet he could imagine the action so well just standing there

a template of light metal
hanging by the bale press caught his eye
the black ink-stained outline
LEOPARDWOOD
he wondered how many bales
merino fibre the large stencil had been used to proudly stamp
questioned if it would ever be used again

as impressive as the whole set-up was
all objects large and small
supported what he thought to be an unsustainable thing
yet it seemed such a shame
there he was
having never before seen the shed in action
somehow wanting it to hum alive again

totally convinced that the property needed a break
from sheep and cattle too
yet feeling such nostalgia walking across those boards
walking out a door at the shed's far end
looking out across the airstrip damp yet well maintained
the empty hangar nearby
everything on such a large scale

the hand of man
had so clearly made its mark in those surrounds
was he wise denying all that was there
all that had been constructed
layered year on year
improvements and expansions
season after season

knowledge about the place
how to farm that particular piece of dirt
contained here
Arthur pondered
what was he going to do with all that
was he going to start from scratch
or learn from what was there and move on

his new vantage point slightly elevated
up on the shed at the top of the stairs
enabled Arthur to pick a fence line
some distance and substance
he could see no end to it at all
straight as it was
along the flat outstretched ground

looking across the expanse before him
seemed that the undulations and the water courses
all things behind him
acacias
plenty of saltbush and the pink soil
almost an orange-red now damp
formed his entire world

21

it was with some pride later that day
Arthur arrived safely home
along a different path from the one taken
he had found what he believed to be the north-east corner boundary
followed the eastern fence line
to what was he guessed a central or thereabouts divider
tracing it back eventually to the shearing shed

from there a different track again
that he sensed headed in the right direction
and he was almost exact
emerging onto a track that lead all the way to the main homestead
what he had seen that morning
in those hours rambling as he chose across the property
at times took his breath clear away

the birdlife alone something to see
even so soon
since the end of the rain
he was convinced that there was a hint of green
patches
ready to spread over the coming days
into a scene of absolute verdure

at one stage he stopped the bike
just to watch a large flock of red-tailed cockatoos
descend and feed on a small group of trees
scarlet flashes at the end of tails
against their uniform black
a staggering sight
as if a painting in oils before him

then there were the two wedge-tailed eagles
encountered feasting on the rank carcass of a ewe
no hint at taking flight as he rode quite close
instead standing upright
tall as himself straddling his dirt bike
resolutely stared him away
as they might a crow or a square-tailed kite

passing by as slowly as he could
without actually coming to a halt
the wonder of being close to their power so raw
more than compensating for the stench
the flesh dead on the ground
eagles' eyes for a moment he was sure
meeting his own

not an easy ride
lots of sticky sections
patches slippery
yet even with his basic skills
and at low speeds
he had managed to make it through
wherever he chose to go

the sore wrist feeling stiff
tired when retrieved from the protective glove
though perhaps no further damage done from the ride
a sense of minor accomplishment came
a positive wave surprised him
having by himself now gained a greater feel for the place
property that he so bizarrely owned

and all without mishap too
he had left the bull at the gate behind
imagined Beth would think that okay too
as he switched off his bike
another engine hum replaced the silence that he expected
that he had looked forward to
the generator purring along effortlessly

Arthur knew that it was not due to him
he stepped across to the kitchen
to the nearest light switch
sure enough electricity again
a further surprise was a full bottle of rum
in the middle of the kitchen table
pinning down a handwritten note was a small phone

from the doorway he could read
a large simple signature at the bottom of the single sheet of paper
Callum
Arthur picked it up
holding the bottle in one hand as he read
hey Arthur
not sure where you are

trust that all is well
notice your bike is gone
we were a bit anxious about you being out here alone
especially as Harry knew about the power
your power will be out for a few days
so I thought I'd try to get through on Harry's bike
and it wasn't too bad mostly

the phone is from Harry
just in case you need anything
if you want you could try your luck
following my tracks back to the pub
but only if you really want to
I used a fair bit of local knowledge
still a bit grim in parts

maybe leave it a day or two eh
give us a call at the pub when you get this
just to check-in eh
remember that Harry got service up on top of the reservoir
I kicked the generator in the guts for you too
hope you don't mind
needs to run for a few hours

Arthur could not have had better news
already feeling good about the morning spent
now a huge anxiety resolved
and friends who were clearly thinking of him
though the bottle of rum was troubling
he could picture them at the bar buying it
a kind of comfort but a challenge just the same

knowing that he spoke of giving it away
the whole thing made him smile
but also came with some upset
his friends clearly did not know how hard
how tough each yard away from the stuff was to make
he would prefer their help in that
not further temptations presented

he couldn't blame them though
it was all they knew
looking at the weighty thing in his hand
he resolved to stash it somewhere out of sight
perhaps eventually out of mind
and so walked over to the deep freeze
placed it at bottom beneath the several loaves of hard cold bread

a funny kind of relief
closing the lid down shut
grabbing up his helmet and gloves once more
Harry's phone shoved down deep in his jeans pocket
Arthur wondered how Harry had felt
a few days before
standing up on the rounded boulders of the makeshift reservoir wall

speaking to someone at his power company
about work that had to be done
above the scene of such cultural destruction
strange for Arthur to be there for any other purpose
but to look at
anguish over
the drained reservoir

so he made the visit brief
just to try to make the requested call
the Tilpa pub number was found in the phone
Frank answered straight away
Arthur simply said to let Callum and Harry know
he was okay and thanks also for the phone
he'd catch up with them in a couple of days

as he attempted to swipe the phone off
mistakenly
clumsily
he brought up on the small screen a photo of a river in flood
feeling not totally good about it
but proceeding anyway
Arthur continued to flick through photos not his own

photos belonging to a friend
several of the river at Tilpa
taken he presumed
from the pub's back beer garden
a couple of metres from the top of the bank
an impressive thing indeed
then photos of young Colin

looking shy and uncertain
at the base of the canoe tree
Arthur sat down upon that high rock
in the warm sun
trapped
unable to stop looking at Harry's selected slices of his world
feeling it was wrong but continuing anyhow

a huge number of frames of the canoe tree
though none at all of Uncle Cecil
then a succession of shots
mostly too dark to pick out much detail at all
of the carvings that lay in shadow
he remembered Harry taking many of these
just below him

all the while saying that he wished he had a decent camera there
and that they needed to be documented properly
and quickly
now emerged from their watery enclosure
Arthur flicked through dozens
noticing that there were many of the chain
the damage caused

then suddenly the photos were all of people
a suburban back yard
perhaps Harry's house
perhaps his wife
other family and friends
happy snaps at some kind of gathering
Arthur stopped

though he wished to keep flipping through
feeling increasingly like some kind of voyeur
he switched it off and stood up to walk back down
glancing down to the carvings
looking down along the crude chain to the tangle below
feeling that he should check on their state
since he was there

yet at the same time
didn't wish to be in again alone among them
there were rocks
possibly more etchings still
at the bottom
below all the rotting matter stuck there
as they had walked upon it each time

he worried if the press of boots from above
was not further damaging things of significance unseen below
he walked down and away
happy not to breathe the same still pungent air
within the cavern itself
fearful that even his breath
would further add to the demise so irrevocably under way

22

during the ensuing months of steady work
no rain at all
it had become Arthur's habit
to spend the last few moments of the afternoon
the final crisp minutes of the winter sky
sitting on the stone supports of his veranda
to watch the sun disappear among the clear long shadows

consider what he had actually achieved
in those previous twenty-four hours
one such evening
the fire had been set
inside his small stone cottage
and the notebook long forgotten
from his backpack retrieved

Arthur thought not only of the day just gone by
but of how he would convey that
and much more
to Beth
Beth of the Plaza Hotel
music spilled across the rocky ridge from the shearers' quarters
his former temporary home

Harry had brought another group
spend some time among the stones for a few days
people from the museums and such
had been and gone
after much preparation and delays
Harry had been busy with them
and seemed in the end well pleased

much documenting was complete
experimenting with different ways of preservation
this new party were family
Harry was in a much more relaxed mode
several groups of elders from upstream and down
had during those few months come to stay
varying lengths of time

Harry always attempted to introduce Arthur to all
invariably an awkward handshake at best
the Paarkintji visitor
coming to a place
on their own country
to view a special thing
with no link to this fella the owner in the eyes of the law

in the eyes of the whitefella law
when he did meet them
handshakes nearly always soft
eye contact barely made if at all
then upon returning from the site
after spending some hours up at the ravine
vehicles always filled with tears

especially among those who visited early on
before the first museum crew had cleaned the site up properly
carefully removing the tangled animal carcasses and assorted debris
there was also a deal of anger
heated debate about what to do
yet there were always Arthur noticed
tears

among the women and men
much embracing
as they emerged from vehicles
comforted one another
clung to one another
often without words
as if in a few moments of respectful silence

all that bad business up there
all their innermost knowledge
what in their lives had also happened to them
sisters brothers
cousins family
friends
mob

the music he recognised as Harry's
carrying across to Arthur in the weakening light
the growing chill
both American and Australian
country and western songs
interspersed
with a fair splash of reggae

the group getting merrier since the mid-afternoon
Harry without his son and immediate family
so Arthur expected the music to only cease with the grog
which would not be any time soon
knowing Harry
all happiness though
despite the weight carried in every heart

it was joy
floating across clear crisp night air
to Arthur
who had declined to party on with them
it was joy
filled the air
for the moment that they were there together

such bitterness could be had
retributions possibly planned
amid what those people were learning
coming to terms with on Leopardwood
yet what Arthur deciphered as he went into his small stone house
with a fire lighting the single room
was the sound of dancing laughter

rising to an occasional crescendo
before fading again away
Arthur heard the sounds of people rejoicing in their lives
and it comforted him
alone at his small stone hearth
pondering flames
what is and what may have been

he pulled again from his bag
his small pack so well travelled
retrieved again the small hardcover notebook
bought in Kyoto less than a year before
bought from a lovely soft old man within a tiny store
selling brushes for calligraphy
and paper that seemed to have emerged in textured sheets from the earth

where to begin
where could he possibly begin to describe to Beth
what had happened to him
he had not seen her since his week at the Plaza Hotel
his first letter a small thank you card
left for her at the front desk with a cheque
one hundred thousand dollars to perhaps help her on her way

the thought of that embarrassed him now
fearing the money sent the wrong message entirely
he expected nothing of her in return
yet his genuine thanks for her trust and kindness
would no doubt be misconstrued by many if not all
his first attempt to use his good fortune well
to do some things worthwhile

after several awkward postcards
he gave up trying to maintain contact
instead bought the elegantly bound small book
brown and cream notebook
if nothing else
a memory of those beautiful backstreets
of Japan

not until China
did he begin to fill some pages
by then with Callum and Sam
he figured that it might be a kind of catalogue
some kind of capture of what he saw
that he would one day present
if that day ever came to present to her

yet barely an entry had been made
he had started off well
diligently
for a few days
but since the sky burial in Tibet
decided he had no taste at all
attempting to capture on paper his thoughts and feelings

though now finding the book again
unpacking his things finally
after his decamp over to the small stone homestead room
despite actually wanting to communicate something to her
he baulked at the thought of it
once he sat down with pen in hand
was there a point to it at all

even if he went straight to his new life at Leopardwood
how to adequately record
things he had found
emotions in himself he had wandered upon
Beth
much has happened
and I am so glad to think of you travelling

as you had said
as you had dreamed
he paused
read through his simple words
feeling already some form of therapy
the words would be for him
his sense-making of the world

I have been making a home in far-western New South Wales
a property on the Darling River
as it happened I uncovered some Aboriginal rock carvings
may be quite significant it seems
some wonderful people I have met here
am gradually working out
how I can restore the whole property

badly over-grazed
my first task
try to fix all the fencing
this will give me a chance to employ some local people
which is what I hope to increasingly do
a beautiful old homestead here too
quite a place I have stumbled upon

I have so far hardly begun
tidied up an old attached small sandstone cottage
can at least live there
while I tackle the big house over time
I'll let you know when the first tennis party is on eh
has its own court
like many farms did years ago

a big place
though not so huge for out here
150,000 acres in all
so I am not stuck for something to do
and the rock carvings are a big deal
found them when I drained this old water reservoir thing
some kind of a day that was

someone years before had just drowned them
an easy place to make a dam
up in this rocky gully
it's full-on what has happened over time
and one more thing Beth
no grog or tobacco for three months now
pretty amazing hey

Arthur reread the few lines
unhappy as always with his poor handwriting
wondering what the purpose
even attempting to maintain any link with her
Beth had suggested
he could for a long time mail anything courtesy of the Plaza Hotel
even if she was travelling they would forward it on

he could track her down
if he chose
though he sensed that this might never occur
if he was honest in his intent to help her
it was to enable her to be on her way
a young woman with purpose
he had no business checking in with her again

noting things down to her though
helped him perhaps distil a few things in his own mind
perhaps challenged him to list off the things he had done
or was at least attempting
reading his clumsy summary of the months just gone
he wondered
what was there of which to be proud

the last bit certainly
something that would please both
both Beths in his life
some decisions about health
his body fragile
he had managed thus far
to do a not so easy thing

and the reason he could
the reason he occasionally had the will to act
push those crazy yabbering monkeys away
was that not drinking was a way of honouring her
his wife
he knew that she'd be proud of him for this
and so he worked at it each day

stopping tobacco was perhaps harder still
but since he'd been sick
following that day digging around the blacksmith's shed
he hadn't forgotten the awful weak feeling
a state of being to which he definitely did not wish to return
Arthur felt stronger
sensed that he was now most definitely a stronger man

it was
as he had heard
one day at a time
yet in just a few months
a new strength seemed to have emerged
the physicality of each day
at first a difficult thing

though after about three grumpy weeks
working things out
he turned some kind of a corner
physically and mentally
loving the feeling of clarity
waking up clear-eyed
making time to eat decent meals

he still pulled up tired at the end of the day
but the coughing fits were abating
his day was not interspersed with endless breaks
for tobacco or trips to the pub for more beer
and Arthur was busy
since the first visits from the Aboriginal Land Council
straight after the flood had dried away

there had been a pretty steady line
those wanting and needing to see the carvings
the Leopardwood carvings
as he had heard people speak of them
all that stuff Harry was heavily involved in
and Arthur tried to stay well away
not his place to be

once he realised that there would be visitors back to back
he worked hard to make the little stone cottage inhabitable again
so that the shearers' quarters could be used by whoever needed them
and the plan worked well
Arthur was right there
but not in the thick of every decision being made
things explained

instead he busied himself
working out the best water tank set up to install
trying to re-fence the property
Sid had been good too
coming through with advice on what to do
and gathering a team of men to assist him
Arthur wanted to employ some local people

Harry had helped Sid to follow these wishes
four young men had been at it for a month already
and after spending a week or so with them
Sid pretty much now left them alone
Arthur had imagined working alongside them every day
but this was not the reality
not required

preferring to be just one of the crew
and so preferred
once they were clearly confident in what they were about
to let them get into it alone
a group of young men working on something
and working lots out between themselves
sorting things out besides

interspersed with the water storage decisions
and fencing out feral animals
Arthur was also on another task
a search of kinds
that he hoped would bring some income to others too
the story of the sandstone quarry had intrigued him
since Callum mentioned it during their first visit to Leopardwood

according to Sid
word was that one of the places
this famous Wilcannia sandstone came from
for a time was Leopardwood
had no idea exactly where
but he was sure he remembered some old fellas
a few years before in at the pub talking

yarns about the different things that used to be
and one of them Sid swore
said he'd stayed on after shearing one year
to work for a bloke out on Leopardwood
cutting stone
Sid said that he remembered him laughing
recalling how tough the work was

never thought he'd have been glad to go back to the boards
after a few weeks of cutting and lumping stone
shearing seemed suddenly easy
Arthur was convinced that the story was real
the lovely blonde sandstone of the original homestead
his new home
and some features around the main house from it made

seemed to Arthur's untrained eyes
the same amazing pale stuff
same stone that he saw in the remaining old buildings in town
downstream in Wilcannia
a clearer and pale cream
compared to anything he had seen around Sydney
or anywhere

figured that if there was a quarry there somewhere
may be possible to mine again
lumping stone
hard work but possible
perhaps good for body and soul
and another way perhaps
to employ some more people in need of work

figured that people across on the coast
in the cities
would pay good money
for something beautiful
something different
as they created their dream homes
their private gardens

he felt motivated
the search for some discarded quarry site
also gave Arthur an excuse to wander
explore
crisscross his property in some detail
he mocked up a mud map as accurately as possible
and as well as he could to scale

in the evenings
marked across it the new country covered
after any day when he'd explored some more
had a chance to get on his bike and look for stones
tried to be systematic about it
travelling a small section north to south at a time
noting the state of fences all the while

starting out at the shearing shed
roughly central as it was
doing just as much as he could each time
he liked the search also each time
for the so many other things he saw
the winter sun had been kind to him since the flood
no rain at all

much of the green growth and wildflowers
that had almost instantly
miraculously come to life after the rain
were still there in their different forms
he still encountered the odd stray sheep
and there were goats aplenty
roos and emus also seemed more numerous

as if replenished instantly
compared to what he saw at first
that first quick inspection in the dry
and the birds always blew him away
not just the large spectacular eagles and hawks
but as he rode he would often be almost ambushed
a flurry of small finches or wrens that he disturbed on his noisy way

on the fourth or fifth foray
he stopped the bike to inspect a promising-looking outcrop of stone
north of the central shearing shed complex
and close by a track
a track like them all
seemed as if it had been there for years
though unused for many of those

the silence and the calm of the place
once he turned off his machine
always a thing to enjoy
the cooler months
meant that he needn't worry so much about snakes as he walked
and he more and more enjoyed the walking
exploring slowly Leopardwood

increasingly feeling like his home
more and more he could find his bearings
the further and more often he strayed
ventured from the secure surrounds
of his aged small home
at first anxious each time he headed off alone
like someone at sea for the first time losing sight of land

but then he got to gradually know
different tracks
the main ones
then their offshoots
and where they'd link back together
where the fence lines headed
and intersected

so that even in a storm
a dust storm when it came
he may be able to sail back somehow to shore
as he walked though on that day
a neat horseshoe of mulga trees caught his eye
no other trees nearby
not even a saltbush close

the mulga threw a small arc of afternoon shade
as he wandered down the gentle rocky slope
just to see what he could see
a small family of roos
startled and took off before he got close
and beneath the tight small canopy of shade
the orange earth smoothed by many creatures seeking shade

droppings also of sheep or goats maybe
mounds of it dry and turning to dust
and fresh stuff too
then as he turned to walk back
in a slightly wider arc to his standing blue white and dusty machine
he noticed a curious slight mound in the packed earth
a circle well trodden

perhaps ten metres or so across
surrounded the slight elevation
and at the very centre
the earth a dish shape holding some charcoal
barely hidden in there
perhaps revealed only recently in the heavy storms and rain
emerging after centuries

crikey me
thought Arthur aloud
picturing warriors painted performing
dancing around an ancient fire
he walked around the mound
from a distance respectful
sitting for a moment back in the shade of the mulga trees

he sat and pondered
a shadow flick swooped across the earth before him
a square-tailed kite he found in the air
Arthur gazed again at the thing before him
the simple mound emerging right there
with the feeling in his stomach he remembered from that day
the morning he arrived at that drained stinking reservoir

23

Arthur sat by his fire
by the glow within his old slow cooker oven
within the small stone cottage
he sat uncomfortably
the night he found the campsite
or whatever site it was
uncertain again

sad again
a melancholy
a helplessness
more treasures it seemed unearthed
one comfort the knowledge
Harry would return again soon
and so he could take his questions once more to him

Harry was to bring another group to inspect the carvings
should he take him straight out there
explore this new find of his
this further evidence of the significance for others
this place he wanted to call his home
Leopardwood
Kirinya

in doing so
he would almost guarantee one thing
the sandstone idea would be put on hold
but that should not figure in his reckoning
he chastised himself
despite his own little plans and schemes
he had to acknowledge what was there

whatever he came across
and who knows
there may be more to come over the years
he told himself that these special things
were not his to expose or hide
he should feel fortunate that any heritage thought gone forever
had been unearthed on his property

it should of course be returned somehow
any how
to those who held it dear
yet it ate away at him
during those few days
before Harry was once again there
revisiting the site

convincing himself even more
a place of ancient gathering of some kind
he also figured
even if the pale sandstone nearby
was not the quarry from years before
it could possibly become one now
with that old access track already there

even when Harry's ute was heading up the dusty lengthy drive
he was not sure what
if anything
he would say to him
Harry's front seat was however full
with people who would make it hard
hard for Arthur to disguise a single thing

brought a couple of surprises for ye
beamed Harry as he got out of his vehicle
Uncle Cecil waved and smiled from the front seat
Callum jumped out from the other side door
konnichi wa he laughed
how'd ye be Arthur
looking quite the grazier there mate in your stone cottage and all

or maybe a squatter eh Harry
more like a squatter our Arthur I reckon
Arthur walked across the front of the ute
warmly shook his friend's hand
you taking a long weekend
hell of a way to come for just the night
prompting Harry to jump in

teacher don't forget
always on holidays aren't they eh
Callum replying theatrically
it's been a long hard winter term Arthur
but I made it through
a sincere Arthur
leaned into the vehicle

hey Uncle Cecil
good to see you again
as was his habit
Uncle Cecil sat for a few moments once arrived anywhere
rolling a cigarette and surveying the scene
thought we might teach you a thing or two
about catching some fish in that there river eh

Harry grabbed Arthur in a handshake and half embrace
and if you want to learn about fishin'
well that old fella sittin' in there
the one ye want next to ye on the bank
so then Arthur
what's happening on your Leopardwood eh
you been hunting for quarries I've been reliably informed

all looked to Arthur
but there followed a lengthy and pregnant pause
after a moment even Uncle Cecil looked directly at Arthur
wondering what such silence could mean
Arthur moved uncomfortably from foot to foot
his hands shoved deep down in jeans
he could not recall ever stewing over something as much as this

yet with those three individuals before him
how could he consider anything but honesty
well the thing is he began finally
awkwardly
maybe before we head off fishing
there's something I think you should see
quite a way from here and the river

Arthur led the way on his bike
wondering what conversations would be had in the ute behind him
grateful for the solitude of the bike
riding alone for a few moments more
but he felt anxious for Uncle Cecil also
remembering the effect the first sight of the carvings had upon him
now something poignant once more to challenge all

Arthur had not told them details
only that he thought it was some kind of gathering place
maybe too one of those ovens in the ground
like Harry had described over at Mutawintji
the few kilometres or so seemed to take a long time to ride
stopping finally close to the place
beside the outcrop of blond sandstone

Harry was close behind
as the other three emerged
stretching from the vehicle
Arthur explained that the stone outcrop had caught his eye
and how he then went over
to check out that little group of mulga trees
across the way

they all walked across in a straight line
moving slowly so as to not tire Uncle Cecil
as soon as he thought it could be seen
Arthur pointed out the small mound
the clear indented circle surround
Harry and Uncle Cecil walked over to the space
with Callum moving closer to Arthur to whisper

crikey Arthur
I think I see what you mean
but you've got better eyes than me
I don't reckon I'd have noticed it there
they both watched Harry and Uncle Cecil intently
respectfully
anxious for their reactions

Arthur soon a little surprised at Harry
when after not very long at all
the large confident man
walked straight onto the middle of the mound
scuffed the ground with his boot
exactly where Arthur thought he had glimpsed flecks of charcoal
Arthur Harry called out loudly

Uncle Cecil smiling up at him broadly
ye see those wires
them electrical wires
on those big poles over that way there
Arthur nodded
not understanding
perplexed

how could they be so obviously light-hearted
so suddenly
well that's one of the main lines around here
cuts through your place as ye know
all redone about three year ago now
and I reckon what you've got yeself here
is one of them sacred Western Energy campsites

lovely spot too for three or four men to base themselves
for a few days
good to see that they folded the fire in on itself all proper here look too
Arthur didn't know whether to laugh with the uproar around him
or walk straight back over to his bike and head off home
he instead compromised
with a kind of whimsical smile

an endless shaking of the head
disbelief at his own naivety
guess we can go fishing then gents he suggested gingerly
attempting to break up the endless hilarity at his own expense
the bike helmet and engine roar
welcome retreats for a time
he had so much to learn

24

well Arthur
Harry spoke so that all could hear
as if making his comment a kind of closing word
you're one of a kind I reckon
but none of us could ever accuse you of not tryin'
eh Uncy
Uncle Cecil was sitting back down with his handline reset

just released a fish too small
that be a fact
right enough
he tryin' hard all right
and better that than the other way I say
no shame in mistakes
don't we all make em

a still sheepish Arthur replied
I won't ever be game again
get you to look at anything else ever again I don't reckon
Harry and Cecil together chastised him
don't be thinkin' that way
or we may miss something special for sure
said Harry emphatically

Uncle Cecil
languid in tone as ever
winding in his handline a little
checking that it felt firm
elegant long hands looking as though specifically created
to be doing just as they were
spoke some more

those carvings are special things
but what is also special
is the fact that it were you what found 'em
it might've been someone else see
and how much else has been found
not just here but across the whole country maybe
and not spoken of eh

you found them there things Arthur
and straightaway look
straight up you did somethin' about it
well
I'd be proud of that boy
I'd be proud of that there
till the end of me days proud

Harry jumping up suddenly
excitedly
here we go
I'm on
landing quickly a pan-sized silver perch
yep not a bad one for you too quipped Uncle Cecil
and so that'll be two you got to my six then innit

and runnin' out of time look
sun be on its way now see
let's cook 'em up eh
Callum had given up on catching anything some time before
instead busied himself with preparing a fire
happily fussing with it
in a clearer sandy section atop the high bank

some decent logs had been dragged close too
all could sit around the warm
once the sun began to drop
cold quickly set in
another frost clearly on its way
Harry cleaned the fish at the water's edge with the last of the light
Uncle Cecil smoking watching on

before they all settled in around the already established fire
Harry asked
still on the wagon there Arthur
accepting a can of beer from Callum
yeah and a few months now Arthur replied
after the first week I decided to try for a month
by then I was starting to feel better y'know

healthier again
so I'm now trying for a whole year
to which a gasping Callum replied
full on Arthur
that'd be something eh
what about it eh Harry
give it away for a year big fella

a touch defensively Harry replied
yeah maybe next year
next lifetime maybe
I'm all right me
and so amid laughter Arthur further explained
it hasn't been too bad
not too many times when I thought I'd just have the one

thing is though
I reckon I'm one of those drinkers
one's too many
two's not enough
ye know what I mean
reckon I've known that for years too
me

if truth be known
the toughest thing was that first day
then the second
by the third the physical cravings were weaker still
so then it's just all in your head
and keeping busy
just trying to do good stuff

not hard to keep busy here
once you get going that is
one day at a time
true that is
at least I reckon it is
importance of treating each day just as it is
one day only in which to do your best

be your best I guess
funny thing too
within about a week I reckon
maybe a bit longer
I felt heaps better
almost began to recognise
the bloke emerging in the morning mirror

all listened intently
Callum enquired
tobacco as well at the same time true
Arthur laughed and explained
yeah well
that is hard
leavin' that stuff behind

I shoved my last remaining pouch
nearly full it was too
down the bottom of the deep freeze
where I hid that rum you left me when the flood was on
I don't pretend I'll forget where it is
but at least it's not in me face if it's there
and I feel good though I tell ye I do

Harry suggesting with a laugh
so now both ye vices are on ice eh
that's it continued Arthur
and what I also noticed pretty soon
once I stopped drinking
was time
just how many hours there could be in one day

prompting Uncle Cecil
now ye sayin' it Arthur
white ladies I was on
metho and lemonade
white ladies we called 'em eh
then when I got meself sorted out
well I know what ye mean there by time

after a while well yeah
lots more time for livin'
when I started feelin' strong again
no more grog sick
twenty year ago now me
stinkin stuff
all that time wasted too look eh

fish cooked over coals in foil
daylight gone
chill set in
the whole afternoon had been a release for Arthur true
so fixed on improving the property had he become
rarely had time to just relax and down tools for a time
he had to spend his time well

things were up to him
if he really did want to make any kind of mark on the place
the responsibility of ownership resonated with Arthur
visits to the carvings did not involve him directly
but he always wanted things to go well
was anxious to know of the progress with all
all the many visitors probing

Land Council
National Parks who were in and out it seemed at will
along with the several people already from museums
more importantly he worried about the likes of Uncle Cecil
welcomed there at any time they cared
then he'd got himself into a bit of a state about the sandstone
the new site that all ended in laughter

a new reason for him to feel a fool
yet not a fool by the fire
an unexpected respite
quiet banter between old friends
of which he now felt to be one
a huge and a welcome change
stillness

what do you reckon about Hiroyuki over in Japan
what would he make of this place then Callum Arthur asked
thinking while questioning
folding some burning ends back in on the coals
to which Callum laughed a little through his teeth
the question surprising him
well I reckon he'd spin out a bit at first for sure

just the whole sense of space
the size of things
but he'd love it maybe too
so different though eh
to which Harry asked
so how would you say it in Japanese
Leopardwood

interested to know
also as a challenge
the often teasing Harry
no idea Callum replied blankly
then smiling as he remembered something
but Kirinya is good
the Paarkintji translation is fun

'cause you see kirin is the word over there for a giraffe
plus a kind of mythical creature and also a brand of beer
then ya at the end of the word can mean a shop of some kind
so beer shop is probably what Hiroyuki would christen this place
soon as he was here
kirinya
beer shop

Harry laughed
intrigued by the words
the other worlds known to his friends
ain't language a wonderful thing
ye gotta love language eh
so this Kirinya Arthur
ye thinking any more about what to do with this beer shop

apart from of course the carvings up the way
Harry asked a little more earnestly
ye might have heard people already
the Leopardwood Carvings
Arthur spoke of the plans they had discussed before
cleaning the place up
creating some work for people in the community hopefully

discussed the possibilities of sustainability
totally solar or wind-powered
or both
Callum once again becoming quite animated
the state of the world
how this place was just a drop in the ocean
but it was at least something

a place that could be a great example
what could be done
if some money was available
thoughtfully utilised
you tell Arthur about across the river yet
Harry asked Callum
um not yet no he replied surprised and deflated

Arthur looked at him
perplexed
and so Callum explained
my dad told me the other day
our old place is on the market again
that's all
thought that you might want to know

Arthur's head raced at the idea
then pulled up with a jolt
what all that might mean for Callum
looking at his friend
then into the fire
brow furrowed
heart beating loud

it's a touch over 75,000 acres
if you're wondering
and I reckon because you got this for ten dollars an acre
you could probably offer eight or nine for over there
might as well
Callum proceeded though cautiously
I've not got the money now nor anytime soon

Harry jumped in
always observing
sensing his friend's mood in decline
yeah but hey
your work is important bud
what you do is work on the future there for our kids eh
that's a big thing

Harry paused
he clearly had more to say
knowing Callum's frustrations well
and he had a few of his own
few people like you
lookin' me boy in the eyes everyday at school
expectin' big things from him

that's what we need
kids excited to learn
feeling connected eh
we got lots a kids going nowhere
black and white and all else too
seems like the new rite of passage sometimes
be goin' to gaol

not a big man or woman till you've done some time
well there be no future there
we gotta have a plan
work together on it eh
like the old people
Uncle Cecil
like I learned

any time there was an issue between people
back in the day
you'd sit in circle just like this here
go through it all
take some time
however long
and give time to the other too

see the other point of view
so in that way there
they knew how to honour what they were
who they were
where they been
and together envision some kind of ideal for what they want
both sides I mean

then together work out how to get there
that's all
prompting Uncle Cecil to rise
embarrassed by the attention
impatient to move beyond talk
aagh
too much beer in you already look

grabbing Arthur by the arm as he departed
motioning for him to go too
continuing only to Arthur
just a few paces away
ye just gotta do your best
no matter how them cards fall
that's all anyone can do eh

come a bit further up here along
follow me close by there Arthur
we can't see I know
but I just want to get along the bank here
where there aren't so many trees
so I can show you Kalthi
emu

Uncle Cecil giggled a little at the thought
trying to make their way along the bank
moving away from the warmth of the fire
total darkness
in an attempt to see an emu
he knew that Arthur would be puzzled
and he liked that idea

the pleasure at what he wanted to teach him
this different but very decent man
look up look
can ye see her
Kalthi
up in the sky
and Cecil waved his slim hands across the starlight

broadly in a slow sweep
not the stars
not a shape of stars
look for the black
the black shape
Kalthi
emu

Arthur suddenly saw it
let out an excited *yeah yes I do god it's huge*
seeing the perfect shape of an emu profile
dark amid the black middle of the Milky Way
it looks
Uncle Cecil
like someone's held a template up there of the emu

like a hand against stone
and all the stars have just been sprayed around it
thassit exclaimed the ageing man with verve
that's 'im
and when it comes out real clear like that
in the cold months like this 'ere
well that's when we know

know it's time to go
get ourselves some emu eggs
let's do that one day eh
Arthur eagerly replying
sure thanks
that'd be great
happily staring at the stars

both men content to gaze for a short while
then a few moments more
Cecil had something else to say
don't you be lettin' anyone pushin' you to buy over there boy
they been drinkin' some this afternoon
as ye know them two
and eight dollars an acre they sayin'

this beautiful land here
all this lovely earth
what do people value eh
I pay twice that every time I buy me tobacco nowadays
what price on this 'ere earth eh
shame I call it
shame

yeah that's right
that's the question
Arthur replied
money eh
I'm wonderin' though
if I won't be asked to move off here someday
maybe that's what Harry's gettin' at in a way

well now Cecil softly spoke
I don't know
lot would need to happen before that be the case
but I won't lie to ye Arthur
what ye found that day when ye drained that stinkin' pool
well
it special that there as ye know

Arthur followed the steps of the older man
fifty yards or so back towards the fire
could hear Callum and Harry talking
though not mindful of their words
thinking through as he walked in darkness
along a soft dirt track
new options before him

sensing endless possibilities
in that part of the world where he had found himself
Arthur trusted feet to sense their way
looked up to the vastness of the winter sky
the sky that in a few hours would turn
turn into a pale blue
amid certain sunshine

where square-tailed kites
circle and swoop their prey
against a pale blue sky and far horizon
where it's possible to see the earth's curve
Uncle Cecil stopped on the soft cool earth of the narrow track
turned to grab Arthur's arm
wanting to say one more thing before they both returned to the fire

keep listenin' won't ye
over there
if ye do go over there
said Cecil pointing across the river
how do you mean Arthur asked
trying to make out the soft face
in the moonless sky

anxious to read his mood
though he could barely see
oh just like ye have been here
listening to the country eh
it speaks to everyone
but not everyone listens
or has the sense to listen seems to me anyways

www.ingramcontent.com/pod-product-compliance
Lightning Source LLC
Chambersburg PA
CBHW071804080526
44589CB00012B/677